The Book of the
STANIER 2-6-0s

By Ian Sixsmith

A British Railways Illustrated Special

First published in the United Kingdom in 2007
by Irwell Press Limited, 59A, High Street, Clophill,
Bedfordshire MK45 4BE
Printed by Newton Printing, London

Contents

Acknowledgements

Primary sources are thin on the ground for freight classes but a few fragments have been consulted at the Public Record Office, or National Archives as it is now. Secondary sources amount to two articles in *British Railways Illustrated*, one many years ago, in which I played some part and a later one in which I played little part; also accounts and references in general works and the enthusiastic notes compiled by the Stanier Mogul Fund. These have been duly pored over; I think I've straightened a few things out (if only in my own mind!) and I apologise in advance for anything missed or if, in attempting to 'unmuddy' the waters, I've only muddied them more. I would like to thank Stephen Summerson, John Jennison and the BRASSMASTERS wizards (purveyors of fine brass models) along with Eric Youldon, Peter Groom, Bryan Wilson, Allan C. Baker (wherever the text threatens to become authoritative in a technical connection, it's usually their notes (admonishments?) to me that are being used, lock stock and boiler barrel) and Jim Norman of the Stanier Mogul Fund. Mention of which... You can join, in a variety of ways, the estimable team whose support for a little black engine with no name transformed her into 'The Mighty Mogul'. Write to the Secretary, Mr. Jim Norman, 7 Chaucer Place, Abram, Wigan, WN2 5QB. *www.staniermogulfund.org.uk*

One of the famous shots of 13245 as first built – the photographic plates, legend has it, were ordered destroyed to expunge evidence of the shocking GWR-style safety valve 'bonnet' or, a bit less respectfully, 'milk churn'. It's a very familiar picture but one which we can't really do without. Note the 'half-cone' boiler parallel between the safety valves and the smokebox, the squared top edge to the cylinders and the crosshead-driven vacuum pump. All the Stanier moguls were built at Crewe but Horwich was the home works for repairs and overhaul. It is worth noting that the Stanier 2-6-0 really came about only because an order for further Hughes Crabs was outstanding. Stanier took advantage of this to incorporate his ideas promptly in these outstanding moguls. If this situation hadn't existed would the Stanier version have ever seen the light of day? Would he instead have made an earlier start with his Black Five?

DRESS REHEARSAL

When William Stanier, C.B. Collett's Principal Assistant at Swindon on the GWR, walked out of the Traveller's Club after a good lunch with Sir Harold Hartley of the LMS, one day in the autumn of 1931, he was looking forward to taking over as CME on the LMS first thing in the new year. At that moment he could hardly have thought that the first design on which he could bring his notions to bear would be a modest and destined-to-be anonymous 2-6-0.

Freight power on the LMS was not nearly as good as Stanier had a right to expect. The Midland 4F 0-6-0 had been widely perpetuated; a good machine, it could have been much better if the axle box bearing surfaces had been man enough for the job. The same failing prematurely terminated the careers of the Fowler 7F 0-8-0s, all the more regrettable for the boiler being an excellent steamer. Similar woes afflicted the Garratts, leaving only the curious Hughes 'Crab' 2-6-0s to shine, relatively, on freight working. In the

Stanier revolution that was coming, the hordes of 8F 2-8-0s and Class 5 4-6-0s would alter this picture beyond recognition, but it was destined to start in a small way.

At heart, Stanier's changes would involve the importation of some basic Churchward design features, duly updated in terms of valve gear and accessibility, and the overturning of some pointless leftovers such as strict perpetuation of ancient wheel centres – though in the case of the Stanier 2-6-0, the Derby 8ft + 8ft 6in crept in under Stanier's nose. He was presumably blissfully unaware of this *totem*.

H.A.V. Bulleid in *Master Builders of Steam* (Ian Allan, 1963) calls the Stanier 2-6-0 'a dress rehearsal' for the introduction of Churchward features, so far as it was practicable. In the months before Stanier formally took up his appointment a small batch of 2-6-0s was in the offing which, in Stanier's absence, would have been turned out as more Hughes Crabs. These would be the obvious starting point and Stanier

duly set to work. The most obvious visual features which transformed these into the Stanier 2-6-0 were the cylinders low down and horizontal, together with the boiler, tapered to allow a steam space without regulator dome. The regulator was in the smokebox, not in the dome-shaped housing atop the boiler; this housed the safety valves/feed clacks. Apparently a measurement oversight or a misreading of the drawings meant the first batch of tubeplates had to be scrapped and Bulleid describes Stanier going 'cap in hand' to the Board, and later putting the Chief Draughtsman Herbert Chambers straight as to checking procedures. After this Stanier moved on immediately to the first Pacifics; Chambers was soon to give way to the now-better known Coleman, whose readiness to embrace new notions and concepts were more suited to Stanier's thinking.

Stanier employed a higher boiler pressure in his 2-6-0 but the low cylinders which this made possible rang

Another new 13245... This is the form arrived at with the 21st loco, 13265 but, as was its wont, the LMS arranged for the identity to be faked. Someone decided a picture of the first one was needed – overlooking the fact that the outline was at the time completely different! This is patently not 13245 and the best guess is 13265, with by now standard boiler clothing, giving a 'full-cone' continuously tapering outline, with round top cylinders. The beautiful picking out in grey and white does its job, highlighting all the detail. At first the moguls had the GWR-type small ejector – visible midway up the firebox just in front of the cab. The vertical pipe connected the ejector to the vacuum train pipe while the pipe running horizontally into the cab goes to the driver's brake valve. By the post-war period these had been replaced by the LMS variety. Note change in cover of oil atomiser valve for the mechanical lubricators with steam atomiser conduit on smokebox side since the 'real' 13245 appeared, feed water clacks to dome and 'pop' safety valves on firebox top.

1

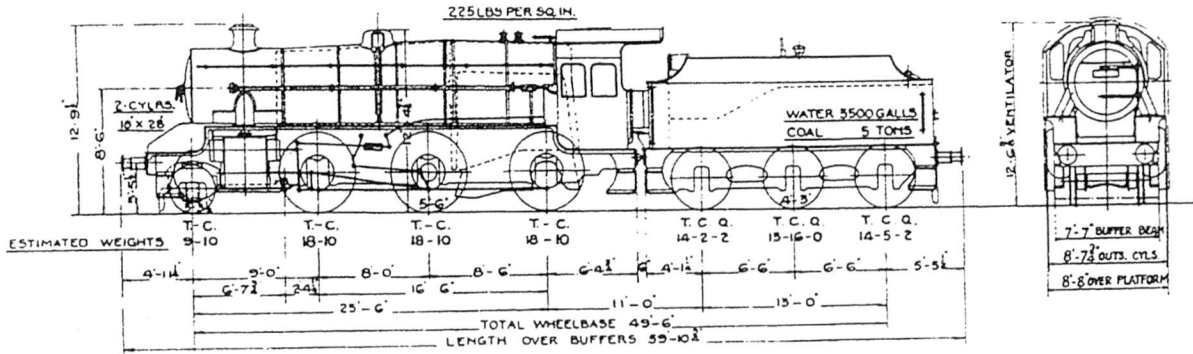

2-6-0 MIXED TRAFFIC LOCOMOTIVE, LONDON, MIDLAND & SCOTTISH RAILWAY.

Official drawing issued in 1934; the version shown has the Stanier hooter – used on the last ten only.

alarm bells in the Civil Engineer's Department – despite the fact that they were some three inches less in width than the Hughes locos. Stanier, however, had the standing and authority, given the straits to which locomotive development had come on the LMS, to cut swathes through pre-existing practice when necessary. In the summer of 1933 three different Hughes Crabs were thus got up with wooden templates to represent the new outline and duly sent far and wide. The reports duly came in, to the effect that the new 2-6-0 would, more or less, happily run wherever the Crab would.

The first Stanier mogul, 13245, duly appeared, less shockingly 'different' than it might have been because it retained the Horwich cab of the Crabs and the same small Fowler tenders. The taper boiler was the striking, distinctive – but above all *new* – feature. No.13245 was notorious too, for the GW-style bonnet safety valve cover mid-way on the boiler, and particularly tall and prominent too. There was time for a photograph or two (much reproduced over the years) before 13245 was whipped back into Crewe to have

Near-final form – for one with square top cylinders that is – with LMS ejector, BR lined black, electrification flashes. Only AWS to come. Crewe South's 42946 is at Stockport Edgeley station, 22 August 1960. Someone was negligent in letting the engine off shed with all that smokebox char on the front, to blow about. Photograph D. Forsyth, Paul Chancellor Collection.

something more conventional and un-Great Western fitted in its stead. The Stanier moguls were all built at Crewe though the Design Office was Horwich, with a degree of assistance from Derby. The several major works of the LMS meant a constant round of vans between them, conveying drawings and parts.

Boilers

Writ small, if you like, in the story of the Stanier 2-6-0s, was the development of the Stanier taper boiler, though whether these changes followed or led developments on other classes is possibly somewhat moot. The various changes (as usual) often overlap in a confusing way but this is more or less how it happened: the first ten, 13245-13254, had a tall dome* (13245's brief

boiler is, in some circles, described as 'domeless' even though they had what was, indisputably, something on the boiler that could only be described, in shape, as a 'dome'. The idea has been that the thing doesn't warrant the name 'dome' because there is no regulator within the said dome. (The moguls had their regulators in the smokebox.) In these books, however, we tend to call a dome a dome; they are the highest point of the boiler for collecting steam; they may or may or may not contain the regulator, top feed, both or neither but, regardless, they are DOMES and would always have the steam collecting pipe.

The boiler had its taper in the first section, from the firebox to just beyond

and parallel thereafter. The dome (or rather, feed water casing) still had the feed clacks to the sides but the (traditional pop) safety valves were now on the firebox top.

The third and fourth ten, 13265-13274 and 13275-13284, had the 'full-cone' taper, from the firebox front all the way to the rear of the smokebox from the first. The boiler underneath remained as before of course. The earlier ones all soon acquired this full-cone outline of boiler. This continuously tapering boiler outline became the Stanier form, so familiar across thousands of locos.

An exception seems to have arisen to this in the shape (literally) of 42955 and with the eye of faith (these matters

For an engine that was short-changed in the aesthetics department, with the 'wrong' (too narrow, that is; no complaints with the side-on view) tender and that 'lowslung' look at the front, the Stanier mogul, in this sort of outline, clearly rises above its disadvantages! But take a look at the boiler outline on 42955 with an 'errant' boiler. Is it straight in the front section? Ribbing on spokes apparent. This is Stockport Edgeley shed yard, 1 June 1960. Photograph D. Forsyth, Paul Chancellor Collection.

'bonnet' aside) with feed water clacks to each side. These had safety valves combined, in Swindon fashion. The dome was open for the safety valves, obviously, but this was only visible from above and, sadly, even fewer photographers took locomotives from above in the 1930s than they did in latter years. The replacement of the 'GW pattern' safety valves on this first ten, by 'pop' valves on the firebox top, was ordered from 1946 and was complete by 1955; by then the boilers had appeared on many later engines as they were exchanged at overhauls.
   *There has been one or two tussles in terminology over the years and the mogul

the said dome (the top feed casing) with the boiler parallel thereafter to the smokebox. All forty Stanier mogul boilers were classified '3D' and this shape was an outcome of the clothing; it was known as the 'half-cone'. Strictly speaking they were not 'cones' because only the top of boiler was tapered, with the bottom being parallel, but it is a useful description for our purposes (only the Pacifics, apparently, had a true cone about the centre line).

The second ten, 13255-13264, had the same half-cone outline of the clothing; tapering, that is, from the firebox front to the dome (the first ring to be precise)

are not always so obvious as you'd think) it can be seen to have retained (or acquired) the 'half-cone' outline later in life.

The mogul 3D boilers had 14 superheater elements and 160 small tubes. From 1939 through to 1951 they were rebuilt to 21 superheater elements and 202 small. Three spares had been built in 1935; the 3D used on the mogul was not interchangeable with any other type.

Stanier initiated a programme 'to meet the requirements for different sizes of boiler with the least number of sets of

3

The Mighty Mogul

Jim Norman has lived with 2968, the Mighty Mogul, for over thirty years now and the following reflections are fascinating indeed:

'...I know the engine has her faults but, then again, what doesn't? The fact is that the class had a poor reputation in BR days, and I'm fully aware of it, though not the cause. When the embryonic Stanier Mogul Fund agreed that she should be saved for her historical importance we had no idea of the boiler or mechanical condition, but decided that, if running order wasn't achievable, she should still be saved and cosmetically restored. We felt that the poor performance would still be adequate for Severn Valley Railway use.

The reality, when she did enter traffic, was a pleasant surprise: crews reported a willing, free steaming, strong and sure footed locomotive. When she went back on the main line in 1996, opinions were expressed that we were mad; the class simply wasn't up to the job. Yet if people were surprised by her performance on the SVR, they were amazed at what she accomplished on the 'real' railway, and that included the Stanier Mogul Fund! She literally demolished these old theories, but they reappear now and then. Comments such as 'One of Stanier's less successful designs' appear less often now, but they leave echoes. Some of these appear in this text; perhaps that's why I'm a little defensive.

Steaming: The Mogul's boiler was more than the prototype for what followed, Jubilee, Black Five and 8F; it was the same in major areas. For instance, the barrel on 2968's SVR shedmate 8773 is identical in all dimensions, save the provision of a dome. The boilers are not interchangeable as 2968 has a vertical throatplate; 8773 has a sloping one. Likewise the entire assembly on 5110, firebox and *sans* dome, save for an extra two feet to the parallel ring, making it that bit longer in the barrel, tubes and so on. If these engines are good steamers, which no-one denies, there is no logical reason why the Mogul shouldn't be likewise. Yet we still read, 'They were poor steamers,' or 'They were rumoured to be indifferent steamers.' I don't know where these rumours started; we aren't told, but it is repeated. There is little documented evidence on this, above that generally applied to early Stanier boilers with 14 elements and 2 inch diameter tubes. The test reports invariably state that steaming was 'satisfactory', the highest accolade to which any engine could aspire, save the unfortunate 2982. The little correspondence from ex-footplateman doesn't, with one exception, mention steaming. This itself is significant; enginemen were quick to condemn a poor steaming class, other faults paling into insignificance! The exception was J.R. Carter describing the only occasion he had a Stanier Crab: 2970 on the Leeds-Manchester Exchange stopper. The row between him and his driver was such that this worthy wanted Jim replaced, and to that end he thrashed the engine unmercifully to run her out of steam, water or both, and so justify his claim. But the engine wasn't defeated, 'She steamed beautifully to a punctual arrival at Manchester.'

The dissenting voice was A.J. Powell (*Living with London Midland Locomotives*, Ian Allan, London 1977). He starts by admitting that he had no personal involvement with the class, but then goes on to give a list of its failings. Amongst these were: 'They had a reputation for indifferent steaming ...the small tubes, at 2in diameter, were much too big for their length...' In fact, this is technically incorrect; the engines would have had the 21 elements, 1¾in tubes by the time he refers to. But yet someone else who did not know the engines was willing to condemn them on hearsay. In preservation, she has shown her prowess, but it was the main line where this was proved. True, there were problems: a southbound run over the S&C and a northbound trip over the Central Wales line spring to mind. But in both cases, inexperienced EWS firemen were warned before the train departed that they had not prepared the fire adequately and would stick. The warnings were ignored.

Alternatively, the northbound S&C run was a triumph, while the two climbs of the Lickey (each double headed with GWR 7325) both tell a tale. From the fireman on the first, Paul Burns of Barton Hill Traction Depot, Bristol: *We hit the bottom of the bank with three-quarters of a glass of water and the pressure gauge on the mark – and when we hit the top, we still had three quarters of a glass and were still on the mark! I was firing against the injector all the way up. Not bad, eh?*

The second was recorded by PSOV (Preserved Steam on Video) and the first camera was positioned on the down side just short of the summit. As this is neared, the feather at the safety valve can be seen to be increasing in intensity. The fireman is nonchalantly leaning from the cab window, moves inside to sound a triumphant blast on the whistle, then resumes his casual pose. Move now to the second camera just beyond the summit. As the ten coach train, which is making about 20 mph, passes the valves are seen and heard to be no longer feathering but on the point of blowing off. The train is seen rapidly disappearing into the distance, the acceleration must be heard to be believed. And this at the top of the *Lickey*!

The 'unreliable' tag is another which doesn't bear close scrutiny. Again, these engines were the prototypes of the Black Fives and 8Fs, and while the shapes varied slightly, the underlying engine did not. The boilers, as already discussed, were virtually identical, but so were cylinders and valves, motion bushes, axle boxes and guides, springs, injectors, ejector, etc. If these were unreliable on the Moguls, it should have followed through to the other classes. You have stated that mileages, shopping periods, etc. were about what would be expected for a similar engine on similar work. Again, documentary evidence against the engines is limited and, as the text says, unreliable engines would have been withdrawn early, yet the first Mogul withdrawal wasn't until 1963. Even A.J. Powell, quoted above, gave ground on this: 'I was always impressed, when studying the mechanical casualty statistics, to see their remarkably good record.' Shame he then adds: '...this was hardly surprising in view of the very mundane work done by this quite modern design.'

Again, 2968 in preservation shows up well. She consistently has one of the highest, and often the highest, mileage of SVR locos, around 10,000 miles per annum. This is more than it might seem; she is entirely restricted to the sixteen miles between Bridgnorth and Kidderminster. Her reliability sees her rostered far more than most other locos, and she's usually first choice as standby for other engines on those rare occasions she isn't out on her own account. Remember that, yes this is preservation, but we're comparing against other preserved engines, including a Black Five, 8F and Ivatt Class 2. And SVR engines are anything but pampered!

The tendency to compare the Moguls with the Black Fives is understandable but not entirely fair, to either class. No argument with the statement '...they could never match the Black Fives across the whole *range* of duties...' except for the implication the Five could always match the Mogul. It's too simple to say that both are mixed traffic locos with a power class of 5; they were built for different reasons and different traffic.

The Moguls followed on from the Crabs, which were built in the understanding of what was needed of a mixed traffic loco in the early 1920s. They were capable of working the expresses of the time, but things change. The LNER upgraded its passenger timings by inserting a few very fast trains among the rest, but the LMS tried for a less spectacular but probably more appreciated goal of raising the standards of all its services in increments. By the early 1930s this was in swing and the Crabs were struggling at the higher speeds. It was into this scenario that the Moguls were launched. They thus never had an opportunity at the crack expresses; they were unsuitable at birth but fortunately Stanier had brought with him the *concept* of the GWR Hall class, although the resultant Black Five owed little to it dimensionally. But its wheels, six inches bigger than the Moguls', gave it a better turn of speed. Unfortunately, at the other end of the spectrum, those extra six inches had an adverse effect. The fact is that the Moguls were much stronger engines than the Black Fives, more so than the reduction in wheel diameter suggests, although we are unable to find just why this should be.

At low speeds, the Moguls were in their element and could easily outperform a Black Five. I'll concede that a driver of an express would always take the Black 'un rather than a Mogul, but with fifty wagons of wet slack it would be a very different matter. They gravitated to the freights, and this was their natural home, where the outshone the Black Five. On fitteds, parcels, locals, excursions etc., there was little to choose, but after that the Fives moved, literally, ahead. Unfortunately, the enthusiast is obsessed by the express, the railwayman knows where the money came from!

A few days out of a Heavy General, 42961 has returned home to Crewe North and worked a job to Derby, where it rests before returning, 3 June 1957. The location looks like the area of the 'North Staffs' turntable rather than the shed proper. You might have thought it would have got the second tender emblem... Photograph R.J. Buckley, Initial Photographics.

flanging blocks' as part of a drive to fit taper boilers to existing LMS classes and what became the 3D would be suitable for the existing Hughes Crabs too; this was never done of course and the 3D remained unique to the moguls.

The original forty boilers were numbered in three sequences and though the Engine History Cards do not note the first boiler fitted, it has been possible to piece them together by cross referencing. The three series (with a fourth for the spares) were fitted sequentially, as follows:
13245-13254 – 6051-6060
13255-13267 – 6071-6093
13268-13284 – 8400-8416
Spare – 9246-9248

Mudhole Doors
Stanier's first boilers had washout plugs only and, to assist washing out, later boilers got mudhole doors, two either side on the firebox shoulders. So the original forty mogul boilers did not have mudhole doors, but the last three spares from 1935 got them. When one of these boilers was fitted to an engine, the firebox cladding sheets had oval holes cut to allow access, finished by the usual dish-shaped covers. When an early boiler was subsequently refitted, the oval holes were fitted with similar

shaped blanking plates. These can often be seen in photographs, depending on the state of cleanliness.

Cylinders
The Stanier moguls had cylinders of two distinct outlines, early ones with a 'squared off' top edge and the rest with a more conventional curved outline. The square top ones were, curiously, confined to the first nine only, though 42949 soon acquired a round set. A suggestion from once-Derby draughtsman A.E. Langridge, published by the Stanier Mogul Fund, that the square top cylinders were for aesthetic purposes, obscuring as they did the unsightly gap between the cylinders and the running plate, is surely correct.

For a more technical exposition I am grateful once again to Allan C. Baker; there is a suggestion, for instance, that the Stanier mogul as first envisaged (or even as first built) had a 2½ inch offset between the cylinder centre line and the centre of the coupled axles, as in Churchward's GW prototype designs of 1903. That is, the cylinders were higher than the axle centres. This is extremely unlikely; see next paragraph. The offset was necessary on the GW 2-8-0 in view of the diameter of the driving wheels, so that the cylinders would clear the

loading gauge. However, for the sake of standardisation it was adopted on the other GW classes, such that only the length of the connecting rods had to be different. However, it was later abandoned on further classes with larger driving wheels and, thus, the centres coincided. The offset has little effect on valve events, as even with short connecting rods it only makes about 1% difference between the top and bottom strokes of the connecting rod, and is well within any clearance volume allowed for in the cylinders. It should be remembered in this connection that the relative positions of cylinder and driving axle centres are constantly changing when engines are running, under the control of the springs and depending on the track condition and the amount of water in the boiler (and tanks on tank engines).

So far as can be ascertained, despite the parallel cylinders the Stanier moguls did *not* have the offset and the cylinder centre line was in line with the coupled axle centres in their normal running position. These engines were all built under one Lot, 104, in one batch and only one diagram was ever issued for them – except for the subsequent half-cone, full-cone messing around with the boiler clothing. This

42963 in a lovely view from the path to the shed at Stockport Edgeley, 20 June 1961. An 8F ambles by beyond. Flush riveted tender attached late on; note AWS battery box in front of cab. Photograph D. Forsyth, Paul Chancellor Collection.

diagram clearly shows the centres lining up, and it is inconceivable that so fundamental a change could have been made in a production period of but five months. And in any event, why would Stanier have adopted a Churchward practice, long abolished on the home ground, at least for wheels as large as his moguls had?

If the idea is that the cylinder position was altered at the design stage, well, there was still no reason for a practice that Swindon had already abandoned, unless it was strictly necessary for loading gauge reasons. Attention has been drawn to the need to equalise valve events but this is of little consequence because, as mentioned above, the difference is very slight. The suspicion must be that somebody at Horwich thought Stanier might like the flat/square topped valve chest cylinder lagging covers, as they did the safety valve cover; in the event, in both cases he did not, and an alteration was made! This would only have entailed a different cylinder lagging profile, and would be of little consequence to production. The cylinder and valve chest castings would be exactly the same; it was but a cosmetic feature.

Sanding
Steam sanding was provided to the front of the leading driving wheels and to front and aft of the middle driving wheel. The rearmost sandbox was under the running plate, the others on top of it in traditional manner. Unlike other Stanier classes, they got steam sanding from new rather than the GW-style trickle sanding.

Atomiser Valve Steam Pipes
It is worth detailing the atomiser steam pipes; features which altered through time, as on a number of classes. 13245-13249 had them angled rearwards at the take-off and they followed the smokebox/boiler join down to the running plate. On engines after this the pipe came vertically down and from 12380 onwards the covers were shorter with more rounded ends. On these last ones there was no pipe visible, for it was re-routed inside the smokebox. The oil atomiser valve (the valve cover changed over time) took steam from the 'wet' side of the header for the mechanical lubricators and most Stanier engines had it here, on the left-hand smokebox side.

Tube Blower Cock
Provided for the shedman to operate a tube cleaning steam lance, this was sited on the right-hand side near the front of the smokebox. It later migrated upwards; presumably this had something to do with the enlargement to 21 superheater tubes.

Top Feed Clacks
The covers to the feed water clacks either side of the 'dome' that was the top feed casing varied a lot over the years. Some were rather flat and angular, others curved and bulbous with degrees in between. And they didn't necessarily come in matched pairs; some engines had one of each.

Lubricators
They carried two mechanical lubricators on the right-hand running plate, one for the coupled axleboxes, the other for the valves and cylinders. On the last five, from 13280-13284, there was only a single mechanical lubricator, the axlebox one. The cylinder lubricator was replaced by a sight feed lubricator in the cab. It was thought of as something of a backward step, an experiment or an accident; as the Stanier Mogul Fund notes point out, these were the only five Stanier engines, of more than 2,000 built, to get this arrangement. It was in fact GW practice, employed at Swindon to the end and apparently giving every satisfaction.

'Cinder Guards'
The little 'cinder glasses', the vertical screens at the leading edge of the cab window, were only fitted haphazardly; a photograph is necessary to confirm their presence.

Vacuum Pump

The left-hand crossheads had the prominent vacuum pumps, in accordance with the practice of the times, after the fashion of the Patriots, Royal Scots and others. Their purpose was to maintain sufficient vacuum to keep the brakes off when the engine was running but it was later decided there was little if any benefit (the small ejector could do the work just as efficiently, without the trouble of maintaining the pump) and all were removed in the late 1930s.

Carriage Warming

Only the first ten, 13245-13254, had steam heat pipes on the front and rear buffer beams. From 13255 onwards the front fitting and its piping was omitted.

Whistles

The moguls at first got a Midland-type upright whistle but the last ten, from 13275, got the (Caledonian) horizontal 'Stanier hooter'.

Tenders

The poor old Stanier 2-6-0 would always look a bit of a plodder – it was difficult to make a mogul look rakish after all – but it suffered unnecessarily from a perverse choice of tender. The Hughes Crabs were lumbered with 'Fowler' tenders, a Midland outline which Fowler, succeeding Hughes before his design could be fully executed, simply passed as suitable. This was an early manifestation of the 'Midland is best' thinking that made locomotive progress on the LMS so faltering between 1925 and 1932 and though it saved the cost of design (minimal) nevertheless had baleful aesthetic effects down the years. It was unthinkingly perpetuated for the Stanier design and though looks, in the uttermost end, *don't* matter in a design as long as it does its job, then it's a shame not to take the opportunity to make things *look* better. But there it was in all its absurdity – yet a second class of 2-6-0 for which the tender was strikingly too *narrow...*

The tenders were assigned in numerical order, no.4514 to 13245 and no.4553, last in the sequence, going on to 13284. Coal capacity was 5½ tons, water 3,500 gallons. More than half the Stanier moguls kept their original snap head riveted tenders to the end while others got similar flush riveted ('flush sided') examples, from Crab 2-6-0s or 4F 0-6-0s. Details such as riveting, edge beading and coal rails can thus vary. Stanier Mogul Fund notes reveal that they were not at first fitted with water scoops. The range of duties, distances and speeds would not, it was presumably felt, benefit from water troughs. There is a clue in the Record Card of 2945 for instance, in January 1944: 'fitting water scoop and top feed clack box connection'. It was in fact far from unknown to have tenders appear with the piping and water deflector dome and tender vents but without the operating gear. This could be added at any subsequent time if water pick-up was deemed necessary. The prominent vent pipes were originally not so prominent; at first they had been sited within the coal rails where they were barely visible under the coal; only later did they migrate rearwards.

Livery/Numbering

The moguls were characterised by a coat of dark grey grime throughout most of their lives but the underlying livery was the attractive mixed traffic LMS black with red lining, followed by the equally pleasing BR (LNW) version. Numbers and tender lettering were yellow or gold (depending on weathering and personal interpretation) with red shading. The L M S on the tender was not quite central but was slightly higher and offset to avoid the rivets. They seem to have kept this more or less unchanged until the Second World War during which any that came up for painting emerged in plain unlined 'wartime' black. In the first years of BR some got BRITISH RAILWAYS on the tenders and at least one, 2951, got the 'M' prefix above the number on the cabside. With BR came the attractive 'LNW' mixed traffic black lined in red, cream and grey with early version emblem, followed after 1957 by the second version.

The sideways view. A Stanier mogul late on, 42956 at Edgeley shed on 9 June 1961. It got this flush riveted tender (probably from a Crab) late on which went unrecorded in the History Cards. Tanks were swopped about on frames and so on, so that 'original' could be an indistinct concept. The preserved Mighty Mogul, 2968 for instance, still has her original tender no.4537, though during restoration the discovery of green paint indicated at least one change of tank in the years gone by. **Photograph D. Forsyth, Paul Chancellor Collection.**

New L.M.S. Mixed Traffic Engines When a class of locomotive, first introduced only a few years back, is developed on the same railway to reach a total of over 250, it may be taken as certain that the design has proved efficient, and when, after subjecting it to a process of modification and improvement the design is further perpetuated, it goes without saying that the operating department as well as the locomotive department will have found every cause for satisfaction. It was in 1926 that the first L.M.S.R. 2-6-0 tender locomotives were designed and built at the Horwich works under the supervision of Mr. George Hughes, then Chief Mechanical Engineer, and subsequently more were constructed at these works and at Crewe, until by the year 1932 the number in service had reached the large total already mentioned. In 1932 five of the engines were taken into the shops and fitted with new cylinders and poppet valve gear in place of the piston valve cylinders formerly used. Mr. Stanier has now introduced a new series of locomotives having the same wheel arrangement, but differing in certain essential details from the original ones. In accordance with the standard practice inaugurated by him as Chief Mechanical Engineer, a tapered boiler barrel with top feed is now used. By raising the boiler pressure from 180 to 225 lb. per sq. in. and increasing the stroke of the cylinders from 26 in. to 28 in. it has been possible to reduce their diameter from 21 to 18 in. and mount them horizontally and lower down without exceeding the loading gauge. The superheater and the water heating surfaces have been re-arranged and the former reduced.

Extract from *The Railway Gazette* of 12 January 1934. The new Stanier moguls, it is clear, were regarded (the *Gazette* got the total in the class wrong) as simply an updating of the 'Crabs'; this was the view of the operating people to the end. 'Compact and generally pleasing' was the verdict of the *Gazette* and, looking at 'The Mighty Mogul' today, who could argue with that?

The original power classification 4F (which didn't seem much of an improvement on the 0-6-0s) was painted on above the cab windows and when an upgrading to the hardly more realistic 5P4F from 1934 took place this was painted beneath the cab windows. By the outbreak of war this had further graded into 5P5F. For all this, '5F' only might be painted on the cabside – see below. BR thought them even more worthy, at 6P5F and this was the officially recorded power classification until the end. It is hard to know what to make of all this, and hard to avoid the feeling that Horwich didn't know either. Despite BR's 6P5F classification, you'll only ever find '5' painted on the cabside. In LMS days at least two, 2949 and 2979, carried a simple 5F while Horwich turned out 42967 in 1963 bearing a '4'! You pays your money...

The first numbering borne by the Stanier moguls was the 13245-13284 series. The general 1934 renumbering scheme (enacted in order to get what were regarded as the 'standard' engines into four-digit blocs) saw these altered to 2945-2984 with BR eventually adding 40,000 to get 42945-42984. In all three manifestations the numbering followed the Hughes Crabs.

AWS
AWS, Automatic Warning System, was widely introduced on BR late in the 1950s and while it has not been possible to get specific photographic evidence for quite all of them, it is fair

2960 at Derby on 26 May 1937, fitted up with indicator shelter. No specific detail, oddly, has come to light concerning whatever the tests might have been in aid of though on that day it worked an afternoon empty stock train from Crewe to Carlisle, usually a job for a Jubilee.

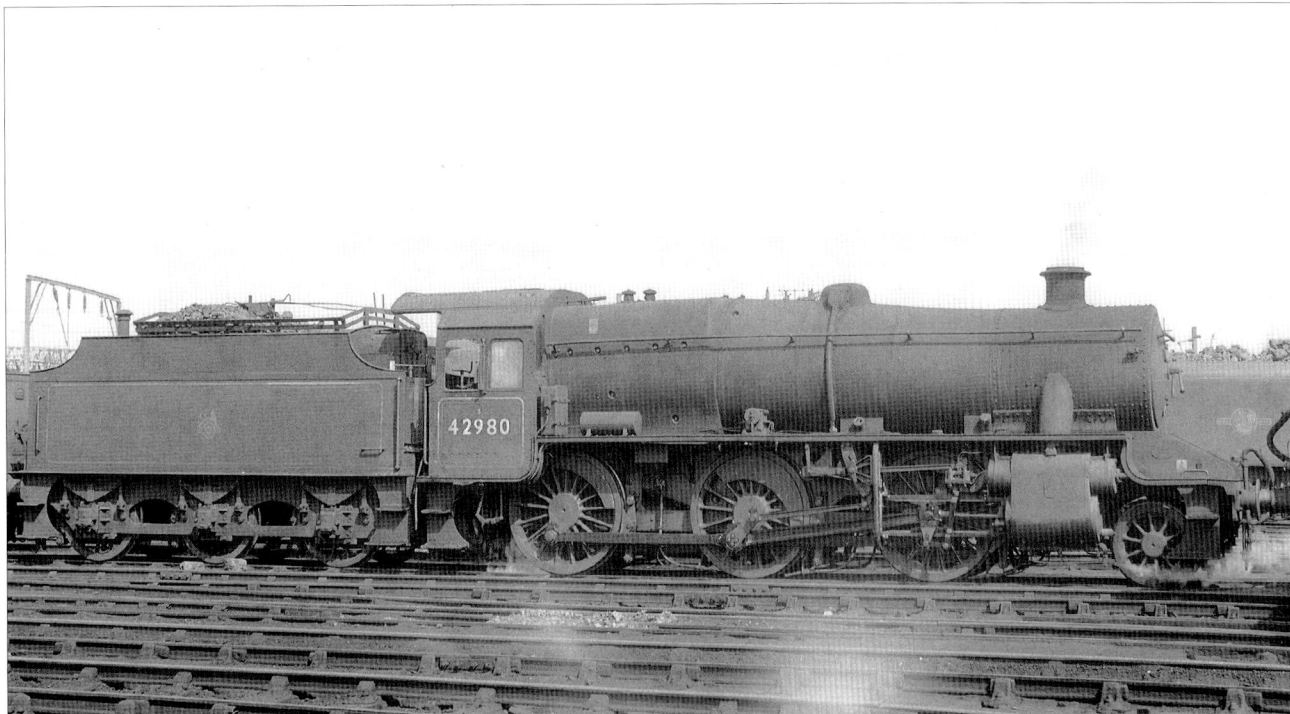

42980 at Crewe North shed, 20 August 1960. The last ten, from 13275, got the celebrated 'Stanier hooter' whistle – the horizontal pipe shown here while the rest got a Midland-type upright, more prominent whistle. Photograph D. Forsyth, Paul Chancellor Collection.

to assume that more or less all the Stanier 2-6-0s got the characteristic prominent protector plate under the buffer beam and cylindrical vacuum timing reservoir and battery box in front of the cab on the right-hand side. An exception, identified by the Mogul Fund, is 42975, though it did get electrification warning flashes. There was a secondary cylinder on the left-hand side running plate, again in front of the cab. An astonishing £400 was allocated for the job – a total, at early 1960s prices, of £16,000 for just one small class.

TESTS

The Stanier moguls were subject to a variety of tests early on, before the authorities moved on to more interesting things. First was 13284 with Hughes Crab 2885, compared in order to see which type might be best for working fitted freights. The trains ran from Manchester to Camden and included a dynamometer car. Through July 1934 both were found to have 'steamed very satisfactorily throughout' and kept time well. Contrary to some verdicts in later years, the Stanier mogul was judged to ride much better

than the Crab. Coal consumption was more or less identical and it was impossible to say if one type was better on the job than another. A more useful comparison might have been between two engines nudging at their next major overhaul, to see how they ran after accumulating high mileages.

The next trials involved two Stanier moguls, on goods trains between Sheffield and Carlisle. In 1934 the cylinders on Edge Hill's 2982 had been bored out by an extra half inch to a nominal 18½ inches diameter, boosting

Perfect illustration of that conjoining of the Crab, the last thrashings of Derby and the Stanier dawn. What followed, the Class 5s, 8Fs and the rest, didn't quite look like this, but the mogul wasn't far off a 'prototype' in looks. The '4' is near-invisible. Crewe South, it is thought, 19 August 1961. Photograph D. Forsyth, Paul Chancellor Collection.

the tractive effort available. The Engine History Card notes the cost at £13 15/-10d. In July and August 1935 2982 was pitted against conventional 2961 (later substituted, because of a fault, by 2954 – then still numbered 13254). The mogul with larger cylinders, 2982, suffered various minor faults which suggest it was never properly readied for the test (in this case you would need one in tip-top condition) and again the outcome was inconclusive. The cylinders of 2982 supposedly reverted to 18 inches a few years later during the course of an overhaul though if they were not worn out it is unlikely that Horwich would have bothered.

42982 indescribably filthy at Willesden shed, on 13 April 1964. This was one of Nuneaton's late acquisitions in which neglect seemed to be raised to an art form. In was in these conditions, presumably, that R. Fox ('Relative Values', *British Railways Illustrated*, July 2002) found one at Nuneaton *with cab and boiler loose*. The boiler, extraordinarily, had dropped to one side between the frames and could *with the help of an appropriate crowbar... ...be moved*. This was presumably the result of a fractured rear end bearer bracket, the repair of which would require a boiler lift and be classified HC, if dealt with other than at a classified repair. An unusual fault (you'd hope) for any steam locomotive; soon, the locomotive would simply have been withdrawn on the spot. Photograph Alec Swain, The Transport Treasury.

At Rugby shed, 29 September 1962; note diesel fuel tanks. This was the last full year in which the class was intact, the first one succumbing the following year. For all its long life, 42964 never got the little 'cinder guard' look-out glass on the cabside. Photograph Peter Groom.

THE RECORD

As pointed out in all the volumes of this series, railway company Engine History Cards, while containing much useful and even fascinating information, are a *guide* to what happened to the engines rather than an absolute cast iron, set in stone, body of statistics. They were, after all, for Accountants rather than Engineers! For instance Works were not above 'fiddling' odd days at either end of an engine's visit for accounting reasons and in any case we cannot realistically expect accuracy to within a day; it was, let's face it, a vast centralised record in pen and ink and simple clerical errors lurk within the record too. It is also daft, in truth, to quote to the precise mile; some of it, for instance, on some jobs, was nominal and some of it (when sheds pinched other shed's engines for instance) simply went unrecorded. As we've said before, mileage calculation was 'honoured in the breach' somewhat and ex-railwaymen will smile when figures are quoted to within a mile! Opinions vary; one camp, the insiders at BR at the time who know what they're talking about, would consider them up to 20% out at least, and almost always on the low side. Others think it rather less, perhaps below 10% for a main line class. For example, when engines were used on ballast jobs, a standard mileage was entered irrespective of what they actually did and how far they went. The point is, however, that the Engine History Cards *tell a story over time* and (this is the secret) the figures *can be compared like for like*, that is from engine to engine within a class and from class to class, for the idiosyncrasies ironed out and equalised themselves over time. If figures were high or low or otherwise massaged, it was the same for every engine.

As with all BR steam locomotives, the record fades from about 1959-60 as it was realised that the old motive power was on its way out. But even the record of the last years show a 'true' picture – mileage *did* decline (often precipitously) as locos sat around unfixed or whiled away the time on pick-up goods or ballasts or were stored serviceable. And, once again it is still possible to compare engine with engine and class with class. Whatever errors there were applied equally to all. Many shed transfers went unrecorded towards the end but the old system of notifying them to the RCTS and others went on, so they can be found in the pages of contemporary magazines and journals. Step forward Peter Groom, who kindly scanned *The Railway Observer* to finalise the shed transfers for the Stanier moguls.

Allocation

Although allocated to the Western Division for most of their lives, the Stanier moguls were well scattered at first. 13245 and 13247 went to Carlisle Durran Hill, 13246 and 13251 to Upperby, 13255-13261 to Kentish Town and 13262-13266 to Leeds on the Midland Division, while 13248, 13250 and 13252 were sent to Kingmoor on the Northern Division. Two or three spent time at Motherwell, 13274 moving on to Polmadie. The Central Division received 13275, 13276, 13277 and 13280-13284 at Newton Heath when new and 13278 and 13279 were briefly at Huddersfield, then Rose Grove between May 1934 and May 1935. All, however, had joined the rest of the class on the Western Division by July 1935.

42945 in final form with 'full-cone' boiler clothing, at Derby shed on 7 September 1953 – it has arrived on a special, 'W72', from its home at Mold Junction. Tender is original style riveted type, with vents inside the coal space, an impractical arrangement that not only encouraged the ingress of more dust but made them subject to a damaging buffeting every time the engine took coal. Photograph R.J. Buckley, Initial Photographics.

THREE LOCOS

ARR		DEP	
	CREWE BASFORD HALL	10.05am D	Day 1
	(04.05 ex-Carlisle)		
4.07pm	WILLESDEN (SUDBURY)		Day 1
	WILLESDEN 58 TRIP		Day 2
	WILLESDEN	7.05pm D (SX)	Day 2
12.53am	CREWE BASFORD HALL		
	CREWE BASFORD HALL	8.00am H	Day 3
9.15am	WARRINGTON	12.55pm H	Day 3
2.0pm	CREWE GRESTY LANE		
	WILLESDEN	3.55am F (MO)	
10.59am	CREWE BASFORD HALL		

TWO LOCOS

ARR		DEP	
	CREWE BASFORD HALL	6.42am F	Day 1
7.56am	MOLD JUNCTION	12.50pm F	Day 1
3.02pm	ALSAGER EAST JCT		
	ALSAGER SHED		
	ALSAGER	7.42am F	Day 2
11.30am	BEESTON	As required	
		Back to Crewe South	

ONE LOCO

ARR		DEP	
	CREWE BASFORD HALL	1.0am(MO) H	
2.45am	MOLD JCT	3.55am (MO) H	
6.39am	CREWE BASFORD HALL		
	CREWE BASFORD HALL	6.20am(MX) K	
		Target 23	
6.45am(MX)	SANDBACH	L.E. (MX)	
	CREWE		
	CREWE BASFORD HALL	8.30pm J	
9.57pm	NORTHWICH	11.45pm J	
12.53am	CREWE BASFORD HALL		

Note: first part of Target 23 covered by a Carlisle engine on Mondays!

TWO LOCOS

ARR		DEP	
	CREWE BASFORD HALL	1.0am E	Day 1
5.0am	LEICESTER	8.15am freight	Day 1
9.15am	NUNEATON		
	NUNEATON - L.E. TO		
	THREE SPIRES JCT		Day 2
	THREE SPIRES JCT	4.15(MX) J	Day 2
		7.20am (MO) empty	
7.35am(MX)	MIDDLEWICH	as required	Day 2
10.33am(MO)			
	CREWE SOUTH		

THREE LOCOS

ARR		DEP	
	CREWE BASFORD HALL	1.42am F Day 1	
	Starts Warrington12.33am on		
	Mons and changes locos Crewe		
4.40am	COVENTRY	L.E.	
	NUNEATON	2.25pm E Day 1	
7.27pm	HOOTON	L.E.	
	MOLD JCT	L.E.	
	SALTNEY	12.50pm H Day 2	
2.25pm	WARRINGTON	5.5pm E Day 2	
6.40pm	SALTNEY	L.E.	
	MOLD JUNCTION	1.0am E Day 3	
4.06am	BUSHBURY	L.E.	
	BESCOT	12.18pm H Day 3	
3.04pm	CREWE BASFORD HALL		

ONE LOCO

ARR		DEP	
	CREWE BASFORD HALL	9.0am K	
9.30am	WHITCHURCH	10.30am K Broxton trip	
11.25am	BROXTON	12.14pm K 'if required'	
12.55pm	WHITCHURCH	1.35pm K	
4.15pm	CREWE GRESTY LANE		

ONE LOCO

	CREWE BASFORD HALL	6.15am K (SX)	
		Target 17	
6.25am	COAL YARD		
	LOCAL TRIPS		
	SANDBACH	7.0pm J (SX)	
7.50pm	CREWE BASFORD HALL		

Also covered by these locos:

4.10am (MO)	CREWE BASFORD HALL-		
	WHITCHURCH	Class F	
6.50pm (WO)	CREWE BASFORD HALL-		
	WHITCHURCH	Class F	
	?cattle		

Left. The diagrams issued for the locos made no distinction between Stanier or Hughes 2-6-0s; they were regarded as interchangeable and to the Foreman they were Class 5Fs and that was that – summer weekends aside. Crews at some sheds referred to them as 'Stanier Crabs'. It's illogical, strictly speaking, but you can see what they meant...

As with any other class of freight engines, much of what the Stanier moguls did went unsung and unnoticed. As a small class, they were probably even more 'invisible' than most. They did most of their work during the week when we were all at school or work. Or they worked at night. Moreover they tended to find themselves in the netherworld of LM cyclic diagramming in which, though an engine always got back, it might not necessarily be the one you were expecting. The Stanier moguls and the Crabs also had a habit of 'laying over' at weekends at sheds that were not their homes, only starting the journey back on the Monday morning. The following examples of Crewe South Class 5 2-6-0 work (no distinction between Hughes or Stanier versions) are representative of the period 1951-1956 and are of interest for a flavour of the work of the moguls.

Works

The Stanier 2-6-0s were built at Crewe, though they were overhauled at Horwich. Doubtless minor out-of-course collision repairs were done elsewhere, such as St Rollox or Crewe or Derby, when a buffer beam might need to be bashed straight again, say, but they seem to have gone unrecorded. An extraordinary outcome was the transfer of repairs *to Swindon* from the end of 1963, along with the Ivatt Class 4 2-6-0s and some (generally Lancashire-based) BR Class 4 2-6-0s. This, it was said, was to provide work for Swindon though no one seems to have stated the obvious concomitant, that it would take work away from Horwich. Steam locomotive repairs at the old L&Y works ceased in May 1964 and steam in any event on the WR had not much more than a year to go. As it turned out only eight Stanier 2-6-0s were dealt with at Swindon; it doesn't sound much but, looked at another way, this was nearly a quarter of the class. Cutting up details are given where known.

Works Codes
HG Heavy General
NC Non-Classified
HC Heavy Casual
LC Light Casual
LS Light Service
HS Heavy Service

These last two evolved by BR times into:

LI Light Intermediate
HI Heavy Intermediate

HO and **LO** are thought to represent Heavy Overhaul and Light Overhaul and are relatively infrequent entries on the Engine History Cards. Work under these headings presumably differed from the others but no definition is known. Can a reader help?

TRO A tricky one this, an infrequent category for which the duration would indicate something akin to a Light Service repair. In all probability it means Tender Repair Only, which also goes for **TO**.

Rect simply means 'Rectification' and typically took place a day or two after a major repair – that is, tightening up bits that had come loose and loosening bits that were too tight. They seldom took very long – often only a day and might easily be undertaken in the works yard.

(EO) was believed to be 'Engine Order' and has been noted so in earlier 'Books Of'. Under it, some jobs seem to have been ordered out

of the normal run of things; it probably, we now think, meant Engine Only, the opposite of Tender Only.

Mileages between repairs have been omitted and we've stuck to the 'annual mileages'. As an idea of the sort of figures and timescale involved, however, this sample from 42970 is fairly typical:

7/5/34-30/6/34**HO**	12,813
25/4/35-13/6/35**LS**	35,653
7/9/36-9/10/36**LS**	76,469
8/2/37-5/5/37**LO**	103,827
11/2/38-21/4/38**HG**	120,808
15/6/40-3/7/40**LS**	53,265
12/4/43-22/5/43**HG**	121,817
9/9/44-14/10/44**LS**	32,951
8/5/45-9/6/45**LO**	50,002

The mileage figure is 'since previous heavy repair', indicating something like 120,000 miles over 4-5 years between Heavy Generals. It is hard now to say how good this was; the Stanier 2-6-0s managed something in excess of 25,000 miles a year and more than 30,000-40,000 in some cases during the first years. That is not much, really, if you regard it 'only' as a job from, say Willesden, to Crewe and back twice a week. But

it seems pretty good to me, really, given the very slow speeds of lower class steam freights and the enormous amount of 'waiting around' during the course of a job.

It is doubtful if any mogul reached the million mile mark for a life mileage; sample estimates are 42945 947,896 miles; 42960 814,986 miles; 42980 862,177 miles. Nothing to be ashamed of here! This and the mileage between Heavies suggests a typical sturdy, steady, strong and reliable freight loco 'driven in to the ground' and then miraculously resurrected for another lease of life every few years. It was the British system, for good or ill, and let's not kid ourselves that some BR main line diesels fared much better!

42945

Built 21/10/33 as 13245
Renumbered 2945 14/12/34
Renumbered 42945 w.e. 10/9/49

Repairs
4/3/35-30/5/35**LS**
23/4/37-27/7/37**HG**
18/10/38-29/11/38**HS**
1/6/40-24/6/40**LS**
19/8/40-31/8/40**LO**
13/11/41-5/12/41**HG**
4/1/43-23/1/43**LO**
20/12/43-15/1/44**LS**
12/11/45-9/2/46**HG**
29/10/47-29/11/47**LS**
3/8/49-10/9/49**HI**
28/4/51-2/6/51**HG**
28/4/51-2/6/51**HG**
2/6/53-26/6/53**LI**
5/7/55-12/8/55**LI**
19/3/57-26/4/57**HG**
10/10/59-27/11/59**HI**
29/6/60-15/9/60**LC**
17/8/61-17/8/61**LC(EO)**
2/62 **classification unknown**
6/64-9/64 **Swindon**

Boilers
	6051 new
19/7/37	6054 from 2948
5/12/41	6079 from 2967
9/2/46	8400 from 2982
2/6/51	6079 from 42948
26/4/57	8410

Mileage
1933 3,639 (4)
1934 44,904 (40)
1935 26,485 (121)
1936 38,667 (51)
1937 32,200 (129)
1938 35,573 (113)
1939 36,546 (91)
1940 35,435 (79)
1941 28,048 (110)
1942 27,568 (55)
1943 32,410 (72)
1944 31,228 (68)
1945 24,928 (83)
1946 27,581 (70)
1947 24,862 (98)
1948 33,399 (44)
1949 27,966 (75)
1950 31,684 (43)
1951 26,742 (75)
1952 28,770 (53)
1953 26,715 (70)
1954 31,395 (51)
1955 26,379 (83)
1956 26,764 (59)
1957 23,300 (79)
1958 28,049 (53)
1959 25,914
1960 21,329
Number of weekdays
out of service in brackets.
Includes works attention,
shed repairs/exams and
'not required'

Sheds
Carlisle Durran Hill
Carlisle Upperby 18/6/35
Workington 13/7/35
Carlisle Upperby 3/7/37
Workington 22/1/38
Carlisle Upperby 16/9/39
Workington 23/11/40
Crewe South 24/1/42
Edge Hill 7/11/42
Mold Junction 26/12/42
Bangor 20/5/44
Llandudno Junction 8/7/44
Mold Junction 9/9/44
Preston 23/4/60
Nuneaton 9/9/61
Gorton 5/12/64
Heaton Mersey 12/6/65

Tenders
4514 21/10/33

Mileage at 12/36: 113,695
Mileage at 31/12/50: 543,123
Withdrawn w.e. 26/3/66
Cut up J. Cashmore, Great Bridge

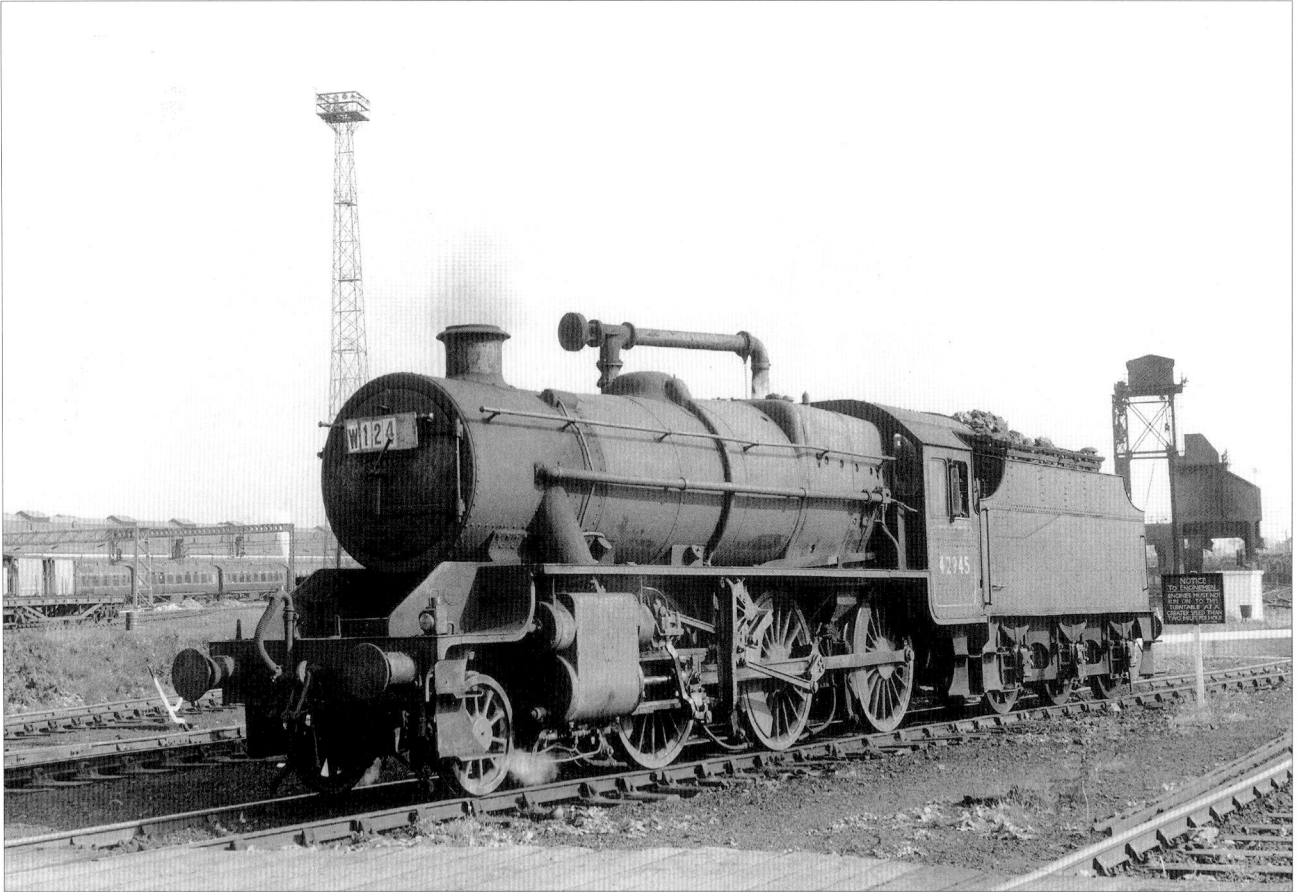

42945 at Crewe South, 22 August 1959. 'W124' indicates the 1.40pm Llandudno-Derby, frequently a 2-6-0 working. By this time the tender has vents outside the coal space. The moguls were repaired at Horwich though a casual observation might suggest they were seldom allocated more than about thirty miles from Crewe. Photograph D. Forsyth, Paul Chancellor Collection.

42946 in fairly clean condition at Kingmoor shed early in the 1960s – AWS and electrification flashes yet to appear. Second BR emblem on tender. The first few in the class had gone to Carlisle, to all three sheds then open in fact; they came and went for a few years but by the outbreak of war were mainly based in or near Lancashire/Cheshire. Photograph J. Davenport, Initial Photographics.

42946

Built 9/11/33 as 13246
Renumbered 2946 21/4/34
Renumbered 42946 w.e. 31/12/48

Tenders
4515 9/11/33
4324 22/3/57
4134 27/5/62

Sheds
Carlisle Upperby
Workington 13/7/35
Carlisle Upperby 3/7/37
Workington 2/10/37
Carlisle Upperby 16/9/39
Workington 23/11/40
Crewe South 24/1/42
Speke Junction 17/11/45
Edge Hill 22/6/46
Speke Junction 20/7/46
Aston 27/8/49
Crewe North 20/9/58
Crewe South 18/4/59
Birkenhead 10/9/60
Nuneaton 16/6/62
Bushbury 21/11/64
Oxley 17/4/65

Mileage
1933 6,115 (4)
1934 50,707 (37)
1935 49,894 (21)
1936 36,779 (89)
1937 39,541 (85)
1938 44,808 (71)
1939 39,067 (88)
1940 39,578 (56)
1941 32,998 (78)
1942 29,373 (36)
1943 27,170 (63)
1944 25,451 (63)
1945 24,563 (51)
1946 18,414 (55)
1947 16,916 (48)
1948 12,881 (80)
1949 22,754 (45)
1950 20,612 (68)
1951 24,606 (22)
1952 23,124 (69)
1953 26,149 (62)
1954 22,309 (75)
1955 23,126 (75)
1956 26,677 (58)
1957 26,466 (37)
1958 22,576 (66)
1959 29,886
1960 20,036
Number of weekdays
out of service in brackets.
Includes works attention,
shed repairs/exams and
'not required'

Repairs
17/9/36-11/11/36LS
25/11/37-21/1/38HG
26/9/39-28/10/39HS
29/4/41-24/5/41HG
17/7/43-21/9/43LS
6/12/44-13/1/45HG
4/12/46-18/1/47HS
10/3/48-5/4/48TRO
4/12/48-31/12/48LS
1/8/50-7/9/50**HG**
25/8/52-4/10/52**LI**
3/12/53-8/12/53**LC(shed)**
29/9/54-22/10/54**HI**
5/12/55-1/2/56**HG**
29/3/58-8/5/58**LI**
28/12/59-16/2/60**HG**
16/3/60-20/4/60**LC(EO)**
25/5/60-14/6/60**NC Rect (EO)**
26/6/61-6/7/61 **NC(EO)**
6/63 **classification unknown**

Boilers
6052 new
17/1/38 8409 from 2977
24/5/41 6078 from 2948
13/1/45 6077 from 2959
7/9/50 6083 from 2962
1/2/56 6055
16/2/60 6071

Mileage at 12/36: 143,495
Mileage at 31/12/50: 537,621
Withdrawn w.e. 20/11/65
Cut up J. Cashmore, Great Bridge

A splendid side-on of 42946, at Horwich on 29 June 1963. Attention has been mainly to the valve gear and cylinders; as at all works, engines in for Light, Intermediate or Casual repairs generally speaking would not get a complete repaint. They would be 'touched up' in the Erecting Shop by painters 'visiting'. Horwich style mounting for expansion link, different from other Stanier engines. Foreground littered with brake crossbeams and hangers. Photograph D. Forsyth, Paul Chancellor Collection.

42947

Built 2/11/33 as 13247
Renumbered 2947 7/11/35
Renumbered 42947 w.e. 30/10/48

Tenders
4516 2/11/33

Repairs
24/9/35-7/11/35LS
6/4/36-14/4/36LO
19/2/37-12/4/37HG
19/5/38-18/7/38HS
24/4/40-17/5/40LS
7/1/42-31/1/42HG
13/10/43-8/1/44HS
12/4/46-15/6/46HG
2/7/47-9/8/47LO
8/10/48-30/10/48HS
30/11/50-4/1/51HG
15/12/52-23/1/53HI
11/8/54-21/9/54LI
16/8/56-10/10/56HG
19/5/58-24/10/58LI
22/3/59-21/4/59LC
20/10/59-27/10/59NC(EO)
13/1/61-8/3/61HI
11/62HG

Mileage
1933 6,025 (5)
1934 50,210 (37)
1935 46,959 (59)
1936 44,873 (40)
1937 37,277 (68)
1938 27,463 (91)
1939 32,627 (29)
1940 25,921 (48)
1941 25,475 (64)
1942 25,689 (49)
1943 17,030 (98)
1944 24,874 (50)
1945 19,447 (87)
1946 25,509 (78)
1947 24,884 (86)
1948 25,293 (77)
1949 27,302 (33)
1950 22,736 (57)
1951 26,530 (22)
1952 25,398 (45)
1953 28,348 (43)
1954 24,489 (77)
1955 28,501 (49)
1956 24,486 (87)
1957 30,532 (32)
1958 22,930 (64)
1959 28,251
1960 26,987
Number of weekdays out of service in brackets. Includes works attention, shed repairs/exams and 'not required'

Sheds
Carlisle Durran Hill
Carlisle Upperby 15/6/35
Stockport Edgeley 22/1/38
Edge Hill 12/2/38
Crewe South 10/2/40
Nuneaton 29/3/41
Crewe South 15/8/42
Mold Junction (loan) 21/8/43
Crewe South 15/6/46
Bangor 28/5/49
Aston 25/6/49
Nuneaton 23/6/62
Crewe South 29/6/63
Rugby 9/11/63
Gorton 2/1/65
Heaton Mersey 12/6/65

Boilers
6053 new
5/4/37 'New'*
31/1/42 9247 from 2955
15/6/46 8414 from 2949
4/1/51 6077 from 2946
10/10/56 6080
16/2/60 6071
was one of the three spares, 9248

Mileage at 12/36: 148,067
Mileage at 31/12/50: 509,594
Withdrawn w.e. 4/12/65
Cut up T.W. Ward, Beighton

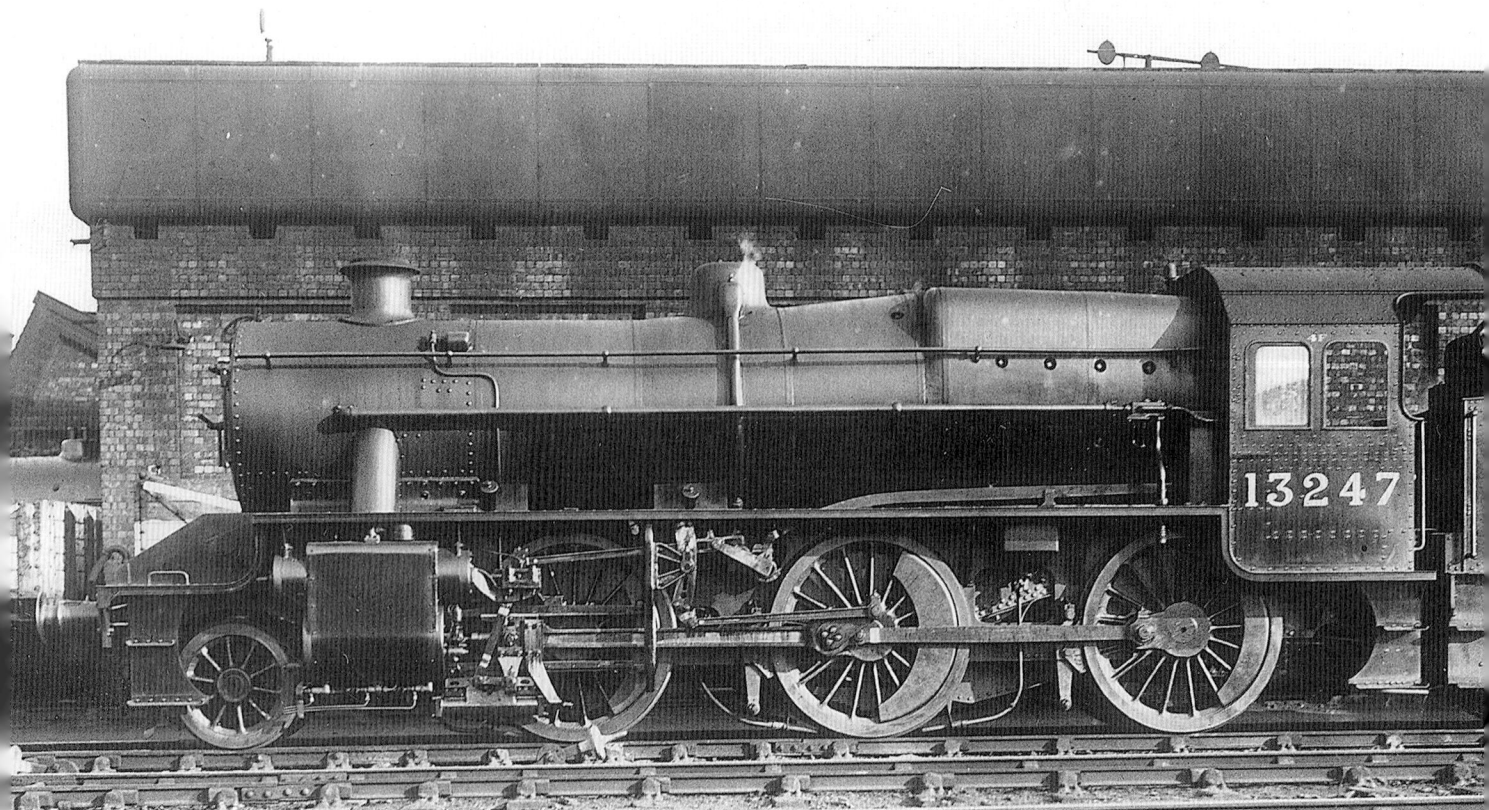

13247 at Crewe South, not long after its construction. An excellent show of that 'half-cone' boiler with the taper restricted to the rear part of the barrel. Crosshead-driven vacuum pump, safety valves on dome, '4F' above window. Photograph R.M. Casserley Collection.

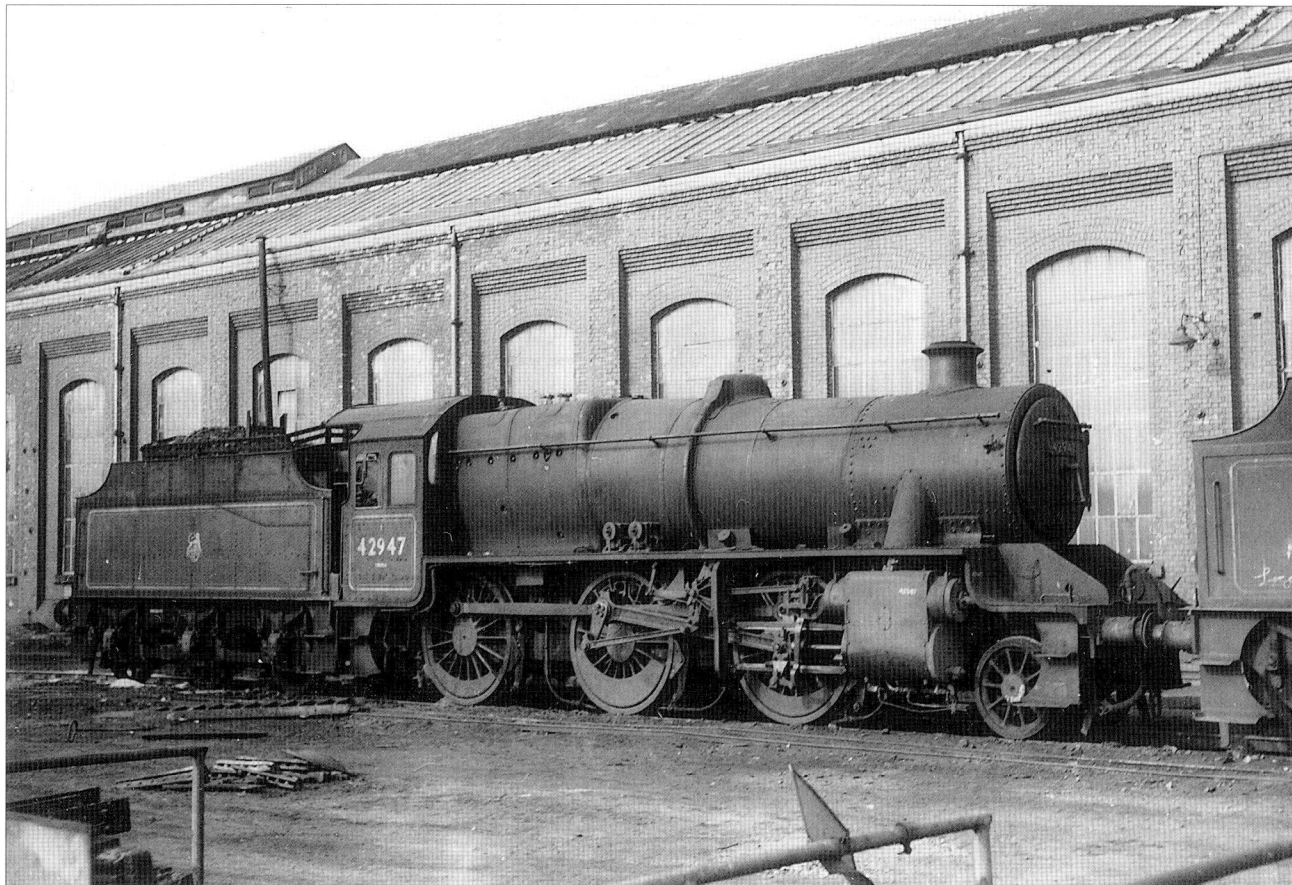

42947 with initial chalk marks, ready for entry to Horwich Works, 5 April 1959. No sign of vents on tender and as yet no AWS. Reportedly, a large part of the Erecting Shop was 'given over to overhauling power cars off DMUs' by this time; memory has it that the work was more to do with EMUs but, whatever, the number of steam locomotives going into the works was severely reduced, to some half dozen a week. Photograph A.J. Cocker.

42947 at Willesden shed on 17 July 1963. This was the year that withdrawals of the Stanier moguls began; already, getting on for a hundred of the Hughes 'Crabs' had gone for breaking.

With tender vents outside the coal space, 42947 is at Bushbury shed, 10 June 1961. It's a good view of the mis-match in tender width compared to the cab. You can hear contrary views on the effects of this; some recall them as draughty and dusty as the wind tore back into the cab while others recall them as no different from other engines equipped with a more conventional cab-tender arrangement. Photograph D. Forsyth, Paul Chancellor Collection.

Second tender emblem on 42948, along with new AWS – note battery box (conduit housing cable prominent) ahead of cab and distinctive cylindrical vacuum timing reservoir – at Stockport Edgeley station on 1 October 1960. While the Hughes Crabs were at first employed in much more of a mixed traffic role, by the time the Stanier moguls appeared there was less scope for this and more or less the only passenger work seems to have been excursions. Once the Stanier Class 5s started to appear in numbers, the moguls became even more firmly entrenched in their freight role. Photograph D. Forsyth, Paul Chancellor Collection.

Renumbered for the first time, Stanier mogul 2948 runs through the medieval style portals at Conway – this is the eastern end and we're looking through the bridge towards Conway. North Wales coast excursions formed one of the regular sources of passenger work for the class. Photograph Paul Chancellor Collection.

42948

Built 10/11/33 as 13248
Renumbered 2948 30/8/35
Renumbered 42948 w.e. 2/10/48

Tenders
4517 10/11/33
4464 2/10/48

Repairs
6/7/35-30//35**LS**
16/1/36-22/1/36**LO**
11/9/36-29/9/36**LS**
8/3/37-21/5/37**HG**
10/8/38-1/9/38**HS**
15/1/40-16/3/40**LS**
27/2/41-16/4/41**HG**
24/6/43-23/7/43**LS**
31/10/44-25/11/44**HS**
17/1/46-2/3/46**HG**
1/9/47-18/10/47**LO**
9/9/48-2/10/48**LS**
4/5/49-4/6/49**LC**
29/1/51-3/3/51**HG**
12/1/53-11/2/53**LI**
19/10/53-14/11/53**LC(TO)**
28/3/55-7/5/55**HG**
4/9/57-11/10/57**LI**
5/11/59-25/11/59**NC(EO)**
1/3/60-5/5/60**HG**
8/62 **classification unknown**

Mileage
1933 5,303 (2)
1934 52,012 (17)
1935 38,873 (93)
1936 42,876 (53)
1937 34,682 (112)
1938 29,980 (44)
1939 35,970 (43)
1940 28,406 (85)
1941 27,853 (80)
1942 36,107 (30)
1943 28,310 (52)
1944 27,468 (70)
1945 33,577 (28)
1946 33,375 (64)
1947 25,667 (111)
1948 28,342 (68)
1949 22,567 (80)
1950 25,549 (46)
1951 21,520 (62)
1952 26,208 (47)
1953 24,214 (68)
1954 25,242 (48)
1955 25,786 (17)
1956 32,440 (36)
1957 27,052 (66)
1958 27,584 (56)
1959 29,256
1960 24,695
*Number of weekdays
out of service in brackets.
Includes works attention,
shed repairs/exams and
'not required'*

Sheds
Carlisle Kingmoor
Carlisle Upperby 13/7/35
Edge Hill 26/10/35
Carlisle Kingmoor 28/12/35
Speke Junction 22/1/38
Shrewsbury 4/6/38
Edge Hill (loan) 2/7/38
Bangor 17/8/40
Aston 25/6/49
Crewe South 26/9/53
Aston 31/10/53
Willesden 5/12/53
Crewe South 8/12/56
Stoke 24/11/62
Springs Branch 14/12/63
Gorton 2/1/65*
Heaton Mersey 12/6/65
*still on Springs Branch
allocation 4/65; almost
certainly never went to Gorton*

Boilers
	6054 new
14/5/37	6078 from 2962
16/4/41	9246 from 2960
2/3/46	6079 from 2945
3/3/51	8414 from 2947
7/5/55	6081
5/5/60	6075

Mileage at 12/36: 139,064
Mileage at 31/12/50: 556,917
Withdrawn w.e. 23/10/65
Cut up T.W. Ward, Killamarsh

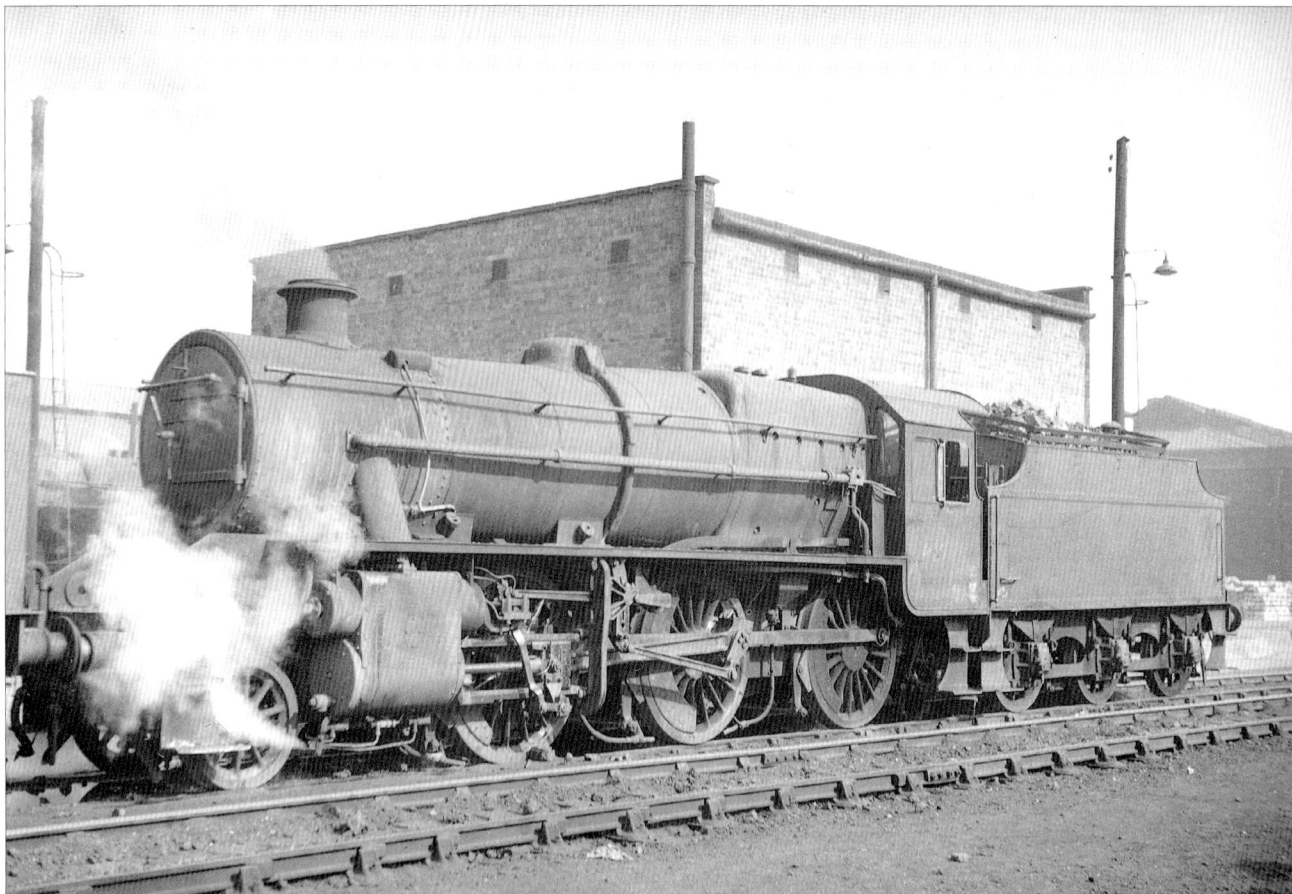

42948 at Willesden about 1955. The class barely figured on the Willesden allocation, especially in BR days but 42948 was one of the exceptions, being based there for three years in the mid-1950s. Photograph J. Sutton, Paul Chancellor Collection.

In much brighter condition, with second BR tender emblem and in almost exactly the same spot, several years later on 25 June 1960. Now a Crewe South loco, its duties still brought it to its old home of Willesden. It is only a few weeks out of a Heavy General but the layers of grime are going on nicely. Horwich has kindly left a stencilled 42948 on the drop curve of the running plate to remind us of its recent overhaul. Exactly what extreme physical forces were expended to get that dart (on the floor) bent like that? Photograph Peter Groom.

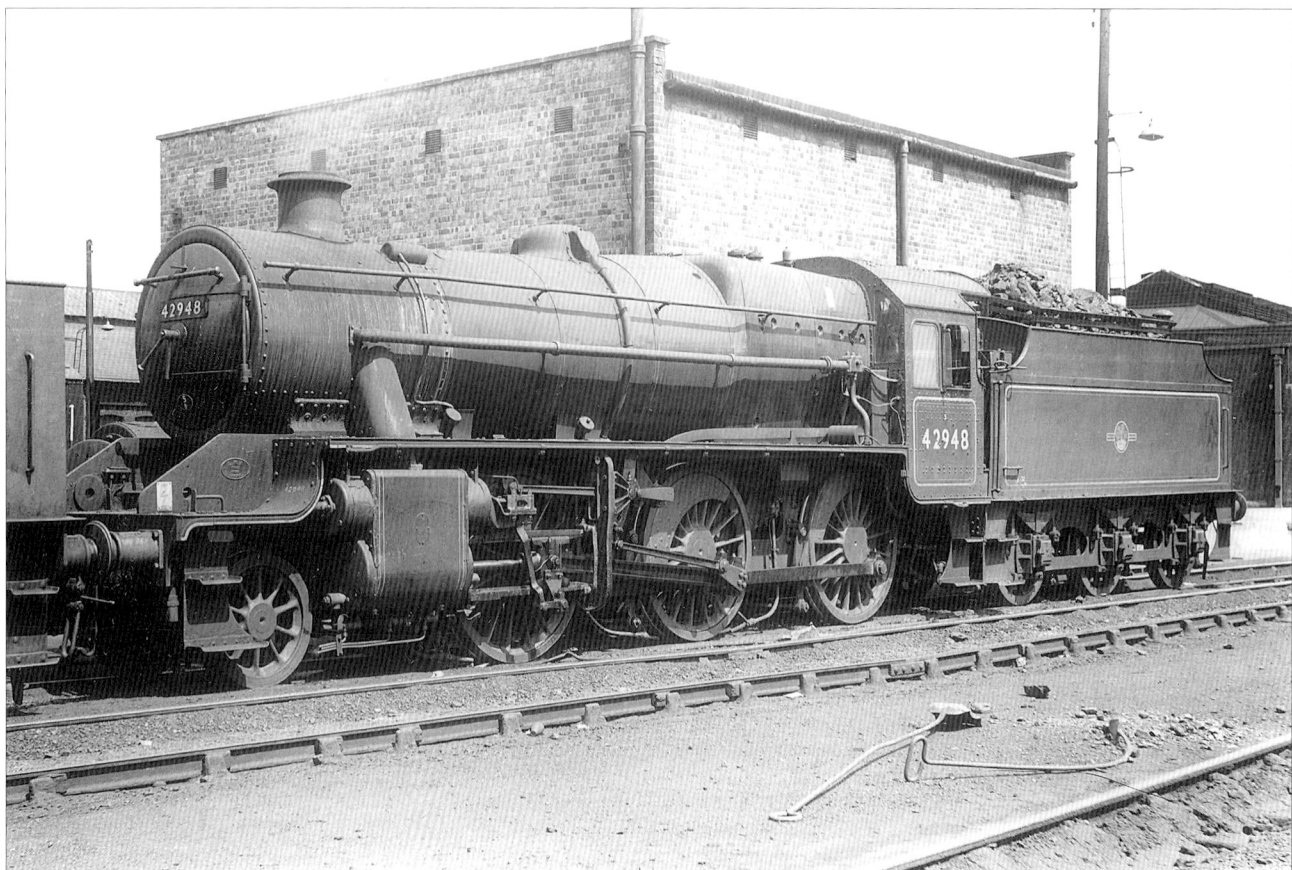

42949

Built 29/11/33 as 13249
Renumbered 2949 23/12/35
Renumbered 42949 w.e. 12/11/49

Boilers

	6055 new
18/11/37	8400 from 2968
8/8/41	8414 from 2966
5/1/46	8405 from 2960
30/11/51	8406
7/12/56	6059

Sheds

Carlisle Kingmoor
Carlisle Upperby 13/7/35
Workington 23/11/40
Crewe South 24/1/42
Bletchley 20/12/47
Speke Junction 6/3/48
Brunswick 8/7/50
Crewe South 14/3/59
Stoke 24/11/62

Mileage

1933 1,151 (-)
1934 45,712 (44)
1935 48,628 (51)
1936 4,942 (72)
1937 36,533 (99)
1938 41,855 (83)
1939 32,107 (126)
1940 31,832 (94)
1941 31,469 (67)
1942 26,491 (43)
1943 25,183 (62)
1944 25,199 (49)
1945 16,280 (119)
1946 29,221 (42)
1947 22,848 (62)
1948 20,694 (67)
1949 19,619 (83)
1950 24,848 (35)
1951 25,543 (87)
1952 34,246 (48)
1953 30,432 (72)
1954 32,740 (52)
1955 33,459 (85)
1956 29,613 (109)
1957 42,921 (40)
1958 36,364 (50)
1959 26,780
1960 24,083
*Number of weekdays
out of service in brackets.
Includes works attention,
shed repairs/exams and
'not required'*

Repairs

15/11/35-23/12/35**LS**
5/1/37-28/1/37**HS**
4/10/37-27/11/37**HG**
27/5/38-8/7/38**LO**
25/8/39-28/10/39**HS**
11/1/40-27/3/40**LO**
12/7/41-8/8/41**HG**
10/12/43-1/1/44**LS**
9/10/45-5/1/46**HG**
24/5/47-21/6/47**HS**
21/10/49-12/11/49**HI**
24/10/51-30/11/51**HG**
13/12/51**NC (Rect)**
9/2/54-10/3/54**LI**
7/3/55-20/4/55**LC**
29/9/56-7/12/56**HG**
5/1/59-26/2/59**HI**
1/11/59-20/11/59**NC(EO)**
15/7/61-4/1061**LI**

Tenders

4518 29/11/33
3966 27/2/54
4532 2/11/63

Mileage at 12/36: 136,433
Mileage at 31/12/50: 522,612
Withdrawn w.e. 9/11/63
Cut up Horwich

2949 in thoroughly work-stained condition, with simple 5F painted on the cabside; tender vents well within the coal space. This would be the late 1930s and even, maybe (the origins of the print suggest) the first years of the war. Note plate with four bolt holes on the crosshead, indicating the fixing for the now-removed vacuum pump. The location looks like Willesden, with the carriage shed in the background.

Early BR days at Speke Junction, 18 April 1950. It was sheds like this, the underpinnings of the vast LM freight operation in the North West, that were the haunts of the Stanier moguls. The piles of clinker seem an almost appropriate accompaniment but the old mogul can still manage a faint dignity, with that half-shiny smokebox. Note buckled front running plate; a not-untypical state to get into. Photograph H.C. Casserley, courtesy R.M. Casserley

The OHL (Over Head Line) masts have appeared as 42949 hurries along the LNW on what would be the Up Fast at Ashton, a village near Roade, 1 August 1963. Vents outside the coal space, AWS. The 1st of August was a Thursday that year and as Stanier 2-6-0s were almost unknown on the southern part of the LNW main line on passenger work it could be assumed that this is probably a pre-Bank Holiday special – though anything is possible of course. The mogul belonged to Stoke at the time; Stoke engines generally were also rarities down this way – she has almost certainly been pinched by Crewe South for this extra job.

42949 with a train at Tiviot Dale station, Stockport, 12 June 1957. This was a weekday, so the possibility of an excursion working is much diminished; Brunswick (the engine's home) had passenger jobs to Stockport but if this is one of them then it's now ended, for the engine is in back gear. The oil atomiser valve of the mechanical lubricators with steam atomiser pipe leading from it is prominent on the smokebox side. It took steam from the 'wet' side of the header and most Stanier engines had it in this place, or thereabouts. Splendidly turned out for a lowly mogul! Photograph J. Sutton, Paul Chancellor Collection.

42949 at Horwich, in for fitting AWS by the look of it – the screw link coupling is still to be put back on at the front. Only the first ten had steam heat pipes on both front and rear buffer beams. From 13255 onwards the front fitting and its piping was omitted. It might be thought that Horwich would simply leave off the steam heat pipes at the front and cap them off as and when the ten went through works. This one, of course, as one of the first nine, originally had square cylinder casings but acquired a round set in the 1930s. Photograph Paul Chancellor Collection.

42950

Built 5/12/33 as 13250
Renumbered 2950 20/11/35
Renumbered 42950 w.e.12/2/49

Tenders
4519 5/12/33

Repairs
26/10/35-20/11/35**LS**
1/1/37-4/2/37**LS**
24/2/38-7/5/38**HG**
27/1/39-18/3/39**HS**
4/2/41-1/3/41**LS**
20/10/42-23/1/43**HG**
18/9/44-28/10/44**HS**
29/8/46-5/10/46**HS**
2/11/48-12/2/49**HG**
24/2/49-25/2/49**Rect**
26/3/49-29/3/49 **'No Report'**
3/10/50-26/10/50**LI**
4/12/50-19/12/50**LC**
12/3/51-7/4/51**HC**
12/1/53-19/2/53**HI**
16/8/54-13/10/54**HG**
22/11/56-21/12/56**HI**
2/2/59-8/4/59**HG**
8/7/61-7/9/61**HI**
10/63 **classification unknown**

Mileage
1933 2,126 (4)
1934 51,825 (52)
1935 45,393 (59)
1936 48,814 (34)
1937 41,383 (75)
1938 34,560 (87)
1939 40,480 (80)
1940 36,327 (57)
1941 25,618 (55)
1942 23,278 (82)
1943 24,627 (48)
1944 22,479 (84)
1945 23,826 (63)
1946 22,979 (77)
1947 31,276 (41)
1948 21,469 (104)
1949 27,164 (75)
1950 24,379 (68)
1951 25,418 (66)
1952 30,986 (36)
1953 28,497 (53)
1954 25,023 (85)
1955 32,730 (47)
1956 29,255 (62)
1957 34,631 (40)
1958 30,117 (65)
1959 29,649
1960 26,351
Number of weekdays
out of service in brackets.
Includes works attention,
shed repairs/exams and
'not required'

Boilers
      6056 new
20/4/38 6059 from 2953
23/1/43 8401 from 2963
12/2/49 6051 from 42983
13/10/54 8401
8/4/59 8407

Sheds
Carlisle Kingmoor
Carlisle Upperby 13/7/35
Workington 23/11/40
Crewe South 21/2/42
Mold Junction 12/9/53
Crewe South 21/11/53
Rugby 16/1/60
Mold Junction 4/2/61
Chester 10/6/61
Birkenhead 14/10/61
Nuneaton 16/6/62
Mold Junction 22/6/63
Birkenhead 5/10/63
Nuneaton 26/10/63
Gorton 29/5/65
Heaton Mersey 12/6/65

Mileage at 12/36: 148,158
Mileage at 31/12/50: 548,003
Withdrawn w.e. 23/10/65
Cut up T.W. Ward, Killamarsh

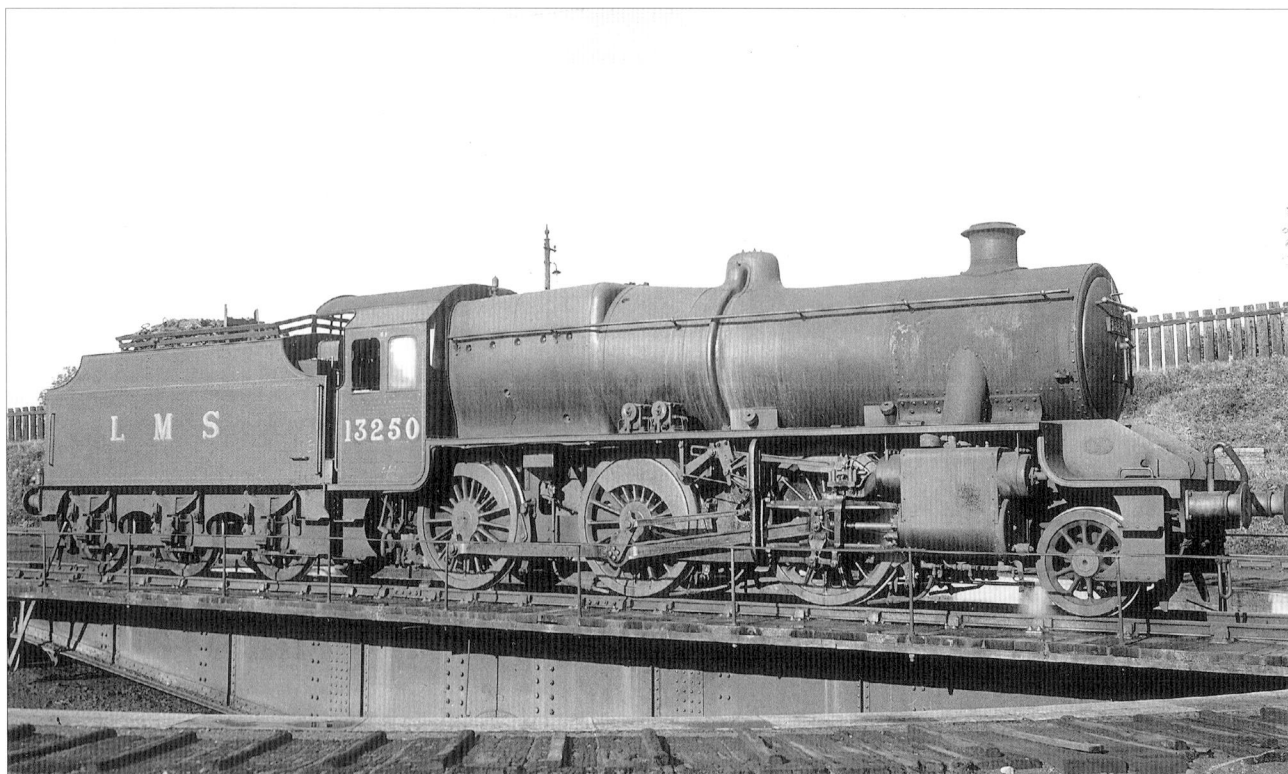

13250 (later 2950) in all her glory on what would be the Kingmoor turntable. The early ones of course had safety valves combined with the top feed clacks in GW fashion – there they are, protruding from the domed casing. The latter, in consequence, is much taller than on the later ones, when the 'pop' valves went instead onto the firebox top, where nature intended them to be. 'Half-cone' boiler and 'square' top to cylinder casing. An all-round perfect portrait. Photograph J.T. Rutherford, The Transport Treasury.

'Full-cone' boiler (or rather boiler cladding) on 2950 now, though safety valves have yet to migrate rearwards. The '4F' above the windows has now become '5P4F' below the windows. It needs the eye of faith but (as with the Hughes Crabs) rain gutters were not present at first where the cab roof meets the side, something which was remedied after two or three years.

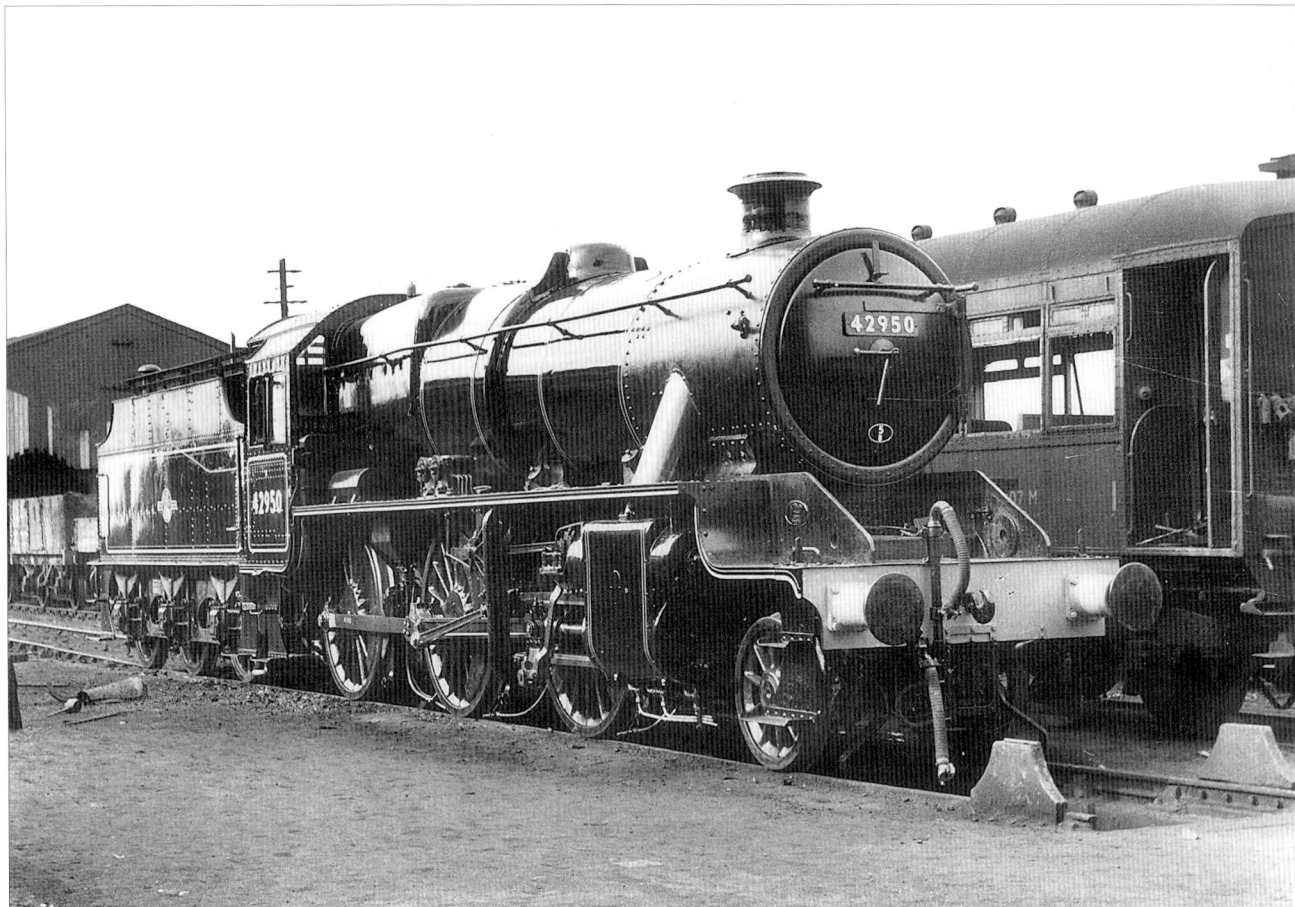

42950 in the works yard (Manchester-Bury EMU stock behind) at Horwich after overhaul, 5 April 1959. AWS has just been fitted. Horwich was the home of the homely, it might be said, getting by on a diet of 2-6-0s and 0-6-0s in the main. Also finished with and sharing the yard with 42950 that day were Hughes Crabs 42732 and 42900, and BR mogul 76035. Photograph J. Davenport, Initial Photographics.

Fully refreshed again and outside the works once more, 2 September 1961, 42950 is on its last recorded visit to Horwich. Now with electrification flashes but tender untouched this time, it appears. One of the 8Fs which were also common fare at Horwich stands alongside; on the Stanier moguls the feed pipes up to the top feed were never recessed or partly-recessed into the lagging as on all other Stanier engines and this is a useful illustration of the contrast. Photograph D. Forsyth, Paul Chancellor Collection.

One of our moguls out on the road, 42950 at Winwick Junction about 1960 with a North Wales-Manchester train. They were the equal of a Black Five on a number of jobs but were never regularly rostered to main line work, in the way that was routine with the 4-6-0s. The space alongside was once a siding, where the engine to assist up Vulcan bank lived. Photograph Norman Preedy.

An up class C freight (typical fare) south of Rugby with 42950 on 24 July 1958. Photograph Peter Groom.

42951

Built 17/11/33 as 13251
Renumbered 2951 11/8/34
Renumbered 42951 w.e. 15/7/50

Tenders
4520 17/11/33
4544 29/9/37
4279 5/5/61

Repairs
11/5/34-9/8/34**LO***
1/1/36-20/2/36**LS**
8/3/37-25/3/37**LS**
17/11/38-10/12/38**HG**
21/2/41-15/3/41**HS**
19/6/43-11/8/43**HG**
15/2/45-10/3/45**LS**
31/10/46-27/12/46**LS**
18/2/48-10/4/48**HG**
17/6/50-11/7/50**LI**
6/8/52-5/9/52**LI**
24/3/53-25/4/53**LC**
14/11/54-31/12/54**HG**
6/1/55-18/1/55**NC(Rect)**
18/4/56-11/5/56**LC**
1/12/56-9/1/57**HI**
24/12/58-18/2/59**LI**
2/3/61-11/5/61**HG**
8/63 **classification unknown**
*'damaged in collision
– no record of cost'*

Mileage
1933 4,352 (1)
1934 36,542 (103)
1935 44,450 (29)
1936 30,916 (68)
1937 34,838 (46)
1938 26,203 (79)
1939 35,693 (26)
1940 28,998 (36)
1941 31,179 (70)
1942 30,262 (24)
1943 21,540 (101)
1944 34,704 (41)
1945 30,341 (64)
1946 29,191 (71)
1947 34,385 (64)
1948 21,218 (101)
1949 26,921 (43)
1950 24,607 (37)
1951 24,509 (37)
1952 24,617 (48)
1953 25,037 (68)
1954 22,484 (80)
1955 26,186 (73)
1956 23,946 (80)
1957 25,549 (30)
1958 24,762 (60)
1959 27,798
1960 27,364
*Number of weekdays
out of service in brackets.
Includes works attention,
shed repairs/exams and
'not required'*

Sheds
Carlisle Upperby
Springs Branch 13/7/35
Warrington 5/10/35
Edge Hill 20/6/36
Birkenhead 25/9/37
Llandudno Junction 20/4/40
Bangor 26/10/40
Longsight 11/10/41
Birkenhead 29/8/42
Bangor 3/10/42
Aston 25/6/49
Nuneaton 9/5/53
Aston 6/6/53
Birkenhead 1/6/57
Aston 29/6/57
Rugby 16/1/60
Nuneaton 21/1/61
Mold Junction 22/6/63
Birkenhead 5/10/63
Nuneaton 26/10/63
Gorton 5/12/64
Heaton Mersey 12/6/65

Boilers
6057 new
10/12/38 6075 from 2959
11/8/43 6071 from 2969
10/4/48 6075 from 2976
31/12/54 6058
11/5/61 8403

Mileage at 12/36: 116,260
Mileage at 31/12/50: 526,340
Withdrawn w.e. 12/3/66
Cut up Central Wagon Co, Wigan

More clumping again, this time for M2951, passing Berkhamsted on 31 August 1949. Photograph H.C. Casserley, courtesy R.M. Casserley.

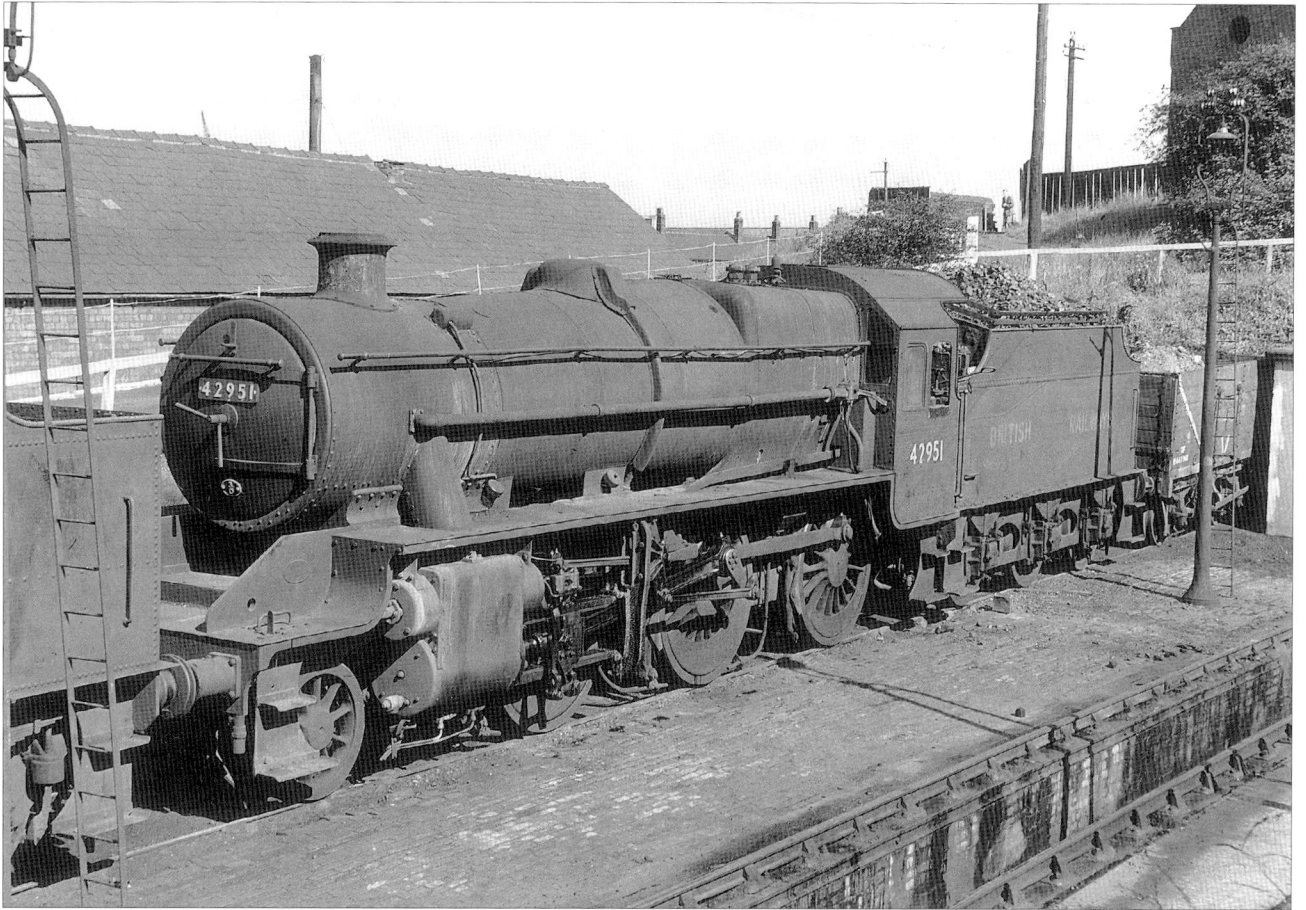

An Aston engine, 42951, at Upperby shed; the date is given as 3 August 1953, though this would be late for BRITISH RAILWAYS still on the tender. Beyond is the cinder path of *Shed Directory* legend that 'led to the shed'. The middle sandbox filler cap has the original style of lid, the forward one has a different type. Either or both might later give way to a lid with a recessed lid – see 42951 at Horwich next for instance. The reason for the cabling along the hand rail is not known; perhaps it's there as some temporary device to measure the steam temperature in the atomiser? Photograph A.G. Ellis, The Transport Treasury.

42951 at Horwich Works on 8 April 1961, fully stencilled up so that all parts went back to the right engine. The other engines are the usual good honest stuff of Horwich, a Crab, an L&Y 0-6-0 and a BR 2-6-0, 76081. Note the narrow gauge track serving both lines of 'inward' engines, originally for WREN and the rest. Successor trolley no.E17 is loaded in this case with rocking grate sections. Photograph D. Forsyth, Paul Chancellor Collection.

42952

Built 21/12/33 as 13252
Renumbered 2952 2/3/36
Renumbered 42952 w.e. 15/1/49

Tenders
4521 21/12/33
4547 31/12/48

Repairs
3/2/36-2/3/36**LS**
31/12/36-14/1/37**LS**
19/7/37-9/8/37**LO**
6/6/38-10/8/38**HG**
10/4/40-22/5/40**HS**
30/5/42-11/7/42**LS**
16/4/43-1/5/43**LO**
10/7/43-21/8/43**LO**
6/9/44-23/9/44**LO**
15/2/46-30/3/46**LS**
3/7/48-15/1/49**HG**
15/2/49-9/3/49**Rect**
26/4/50-13/5/50**LC**
19/6/51-11/7/51**LI**
17/10/52-10/12/52**HI**
15/12/53-11/2/54**HG**
5/4/55-19/5/55**HI**
17/10/55-28/10/55**LC**
29/12/56-8/2/57**HI**
26/3/58-30/4/58**LC(EO)**
30/6/59-21/8/59**HG**
25/8/59-4/9/59**NC(EO)**
7/63 **classification unknown**

Mileage
1933 311 (-)
1934 54,177 (18)
1935 43,422 (28)
1936 30,729 (44)
1937 31,585 (71)
1938 26,451 (96)
1939 25,349 (34)
1940 22,448 (83)
1941 26,868 (37)
1942 25,372 (74)
1943 23,266 (81)
1944 26,276 (49)
1945 23,330 (65)
1946 25,384 (83)
1947 20,066 (107)
1948 11,183 (182)
1949 27,291 (72)
1950 26,171 (61)
1951 26,863 (53)
1952 28,563 (83)
1953 31,274 (48)
1954 30,137 (31)
1955 25,159 (89)
1956 27,224 (51)
1957 29,449 (59)
1958 27,455 (76)
1959 27,791
1960 30,837
Number of weekdays
out of service in brackets.
Includes works attention,
shed repairs/exams and
'not required'

Boilers
	6058 new
10/8/38	8412 from 2980
21/8/43	6052 from 2970
15/1/49	6072 from 2982
11/2/54	8408
21/8/59	8401

Sheds
Carlisle Kingmoor
Springs Branch 13/7/35
Warrington 5/10/35
Llandudno Junction 17/8/40
Bangor 26/10/40
Crewe South 11/1/41
Rugby 16/1/60
Stoke 24/11/62
Birkenhead 22/6/63
Mold Junction 7/9/63
Agecroft 9/11/63
Aintree 23/11/63
Springs Branch 25/7/64

Mileage at 12/36: 128,639
Mileage at 31/12/50: 469,679
Withdrawn w.e. 12/9/64
Cut up Central Wagon Co, Wigan

2952 in a haze at Upperby before the roundhouse was built, when it was a decrepit straight shed, in June 1936. Tall dome with safety valves projecting through.

42952 at Mirfield shed in June 1950, BRITISH RAILWAYS on tender. Whilst the class might have been overhauled at Horwich, the engines did not generally find a home on the Central Division which was, in effect, the old 'Lanky'. The distribution of the Stanier moguls was, however, an early example of concentrating a small class in a particular working area. It was something that could have been sensibly emulated with some of the BR Standards, years later. Photograph J. Davenport, Initial Photographics.

Careering south through Farington station, south of Preston, with a train of brand new hopper wagons. That tender shows up only too well at this angle. The date is not known; 42952 carries a Crewe South shed plate but that is not much use, for the engine (unusually) spent more than twenty years there, from the War to very nearly the Beatles' first LP. The lads look on – would it be a cop? The tall chimney suggested a Jubilee at a distance and the disappointment as a 'Stanier Crab' trundled by did nothing to endear the class to the oiks. Photograph J. Davenport, Initial Photographics.

42952 at Stockport Edgeley shed; AWS conduit sagging a bit. Firebox safety valves very prominent from this angle. Photograph Paul Chancellor Collection.

The usual sorry end, this time at the Central Wagon Co., Ince, Wigan, on 29 May 1965. Final arrangement of lamp irons, top one reduced to middle of the smokebox door, middle one shifted to the side. Either Springs Branch never bothered to paint over its penultimate shed code 8L (Aintree) or it stuck a plate over it and retrieved the plate once the engine went for scrap. At a cost of £4,801 for the engine and £829 for the tender, the final year of depreciation for the Stanier moguls had been noted as... 1974.

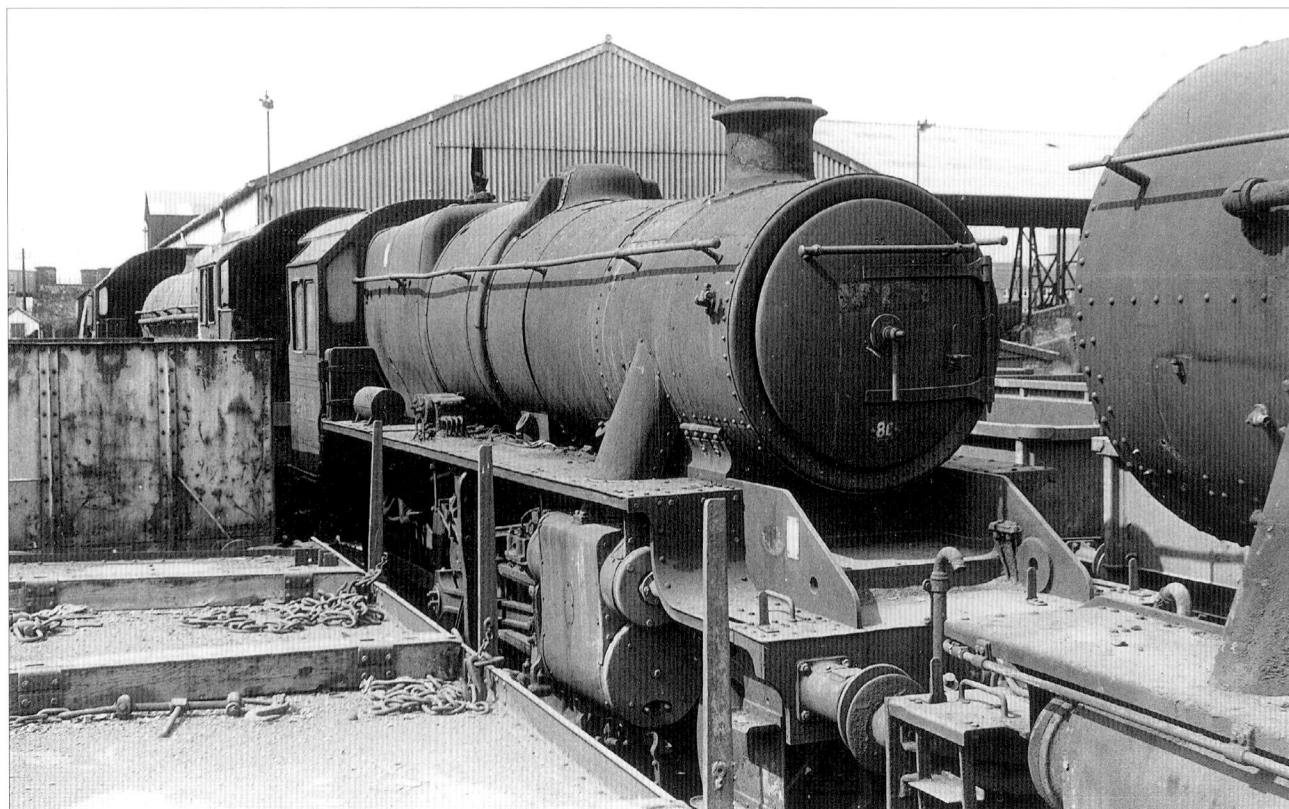

42952 at Crewe South, its home for so long, on 18 August 1962. A good view for once of the 'ribbing' on some of the wheelspokes adjoining the wheel cranks. The little housing with the conduit on the battery box in front of the cab is the fusebox for the AWS. Photograph D. Forsyth, Paul Chancellor Collection.

42953

Built 13/12/33 as 13253
Renumbered 2953 13/4/35
Renumbered 42953 w.e. 26/3/49

Tenders
4522 13/12/33

Sheds
Patricroft
Motherwell 8/4/34*
Carlisle Kingmoor 1/6/35
Carlisle Upperby 13/7/35
Speke Junction 22/1/38
Warrington 29/4/39
Crewe South 21/2/42
Mold Junction 24/7/43
Birkenhead 28/6/47
Crewe South 20/9/52
Crewe North 17/4/54
Crewe South 8/1/55
Bescot 3/8/57 (loan)
Crewe South 17/8/57
Rugby 16/1/60
Nuneaton 21/1/61
Stoke 24/11/62
Carlisle Kingmoor 9/11/63**
Aintree 23/11/63
Springs Branch 25/7/64
*Not on EHC but 13254 'worked fitted
freights to Manchester' (those
were the days!) Remanned at
Durran Hill
**almost certainly
erroneous; probably meant Bolton

Mileage
1933 1,145 (1)
1934 47,106 (44)
1935 31,313 (114)
1936 44,641 (46)
1937 29,408 (87)
1938 24,761 (72)
1939 24,892 (58)
1940 20,705 (51)
1941 22,138 (65)
1942 27,559 (61)
1943 26,461 (77)
1944 33,889 (60)
1945 29,254 (65)
1946 28,072 (75)
1947 21,513 (76)
1948 18,329 (57)
1949 22,676 (52)
1950 20,148 (39)
1951 19,083 (64)
1952 20,886 (63)
1953 30,339 (59)
1954 23,042 (60)
1955 30,355 (53)
1956 28,899 (35)
1957 29,377 (68)
1958 30,577 (56)
1959 30,388 (60)
1960 29,334
*Number of weekdays
out of service in brackets.
Includes works attention,
shed repairs/exams and
'not required'*

Repairs
12/1/35-13/4/35**LO**
23/6/36-14/7/36**LS**
21/12/37-18/2/38**HG**
9/10/39-14/11/39**HS**
13/10/41-1/11/41**LS**
20/11/42-20/2/43**LS**
8/12/44-30/12/44**LS**
22/1/47-15/3/47**HG**
8/3/49-26/3/49**HI**
5/4/51-27/4/51**LI**
18/2/53-4/4/53**HG**
7/9/54-8/10/54**LI**
29/1/57-22/3/57**HG**
5/6/59-9/7/59**LI**
21/10/59-29/10/59**NC(EO)**
12/61-2/62 **classification unknown**
6/64 **Swindon**

Boilers
	6059 new
3/2/38	6082 from 2966
20/2/43	6059 from 2950
15/3/47	8409 from 2955
4/4/53	8405
22/3/57	6078

Mileage at 12/36: 124,205
Mileage at 31/12/50: 474,010
Withdrawn w.e. 15/1/66
Cut up T.W. Ward, Beighton

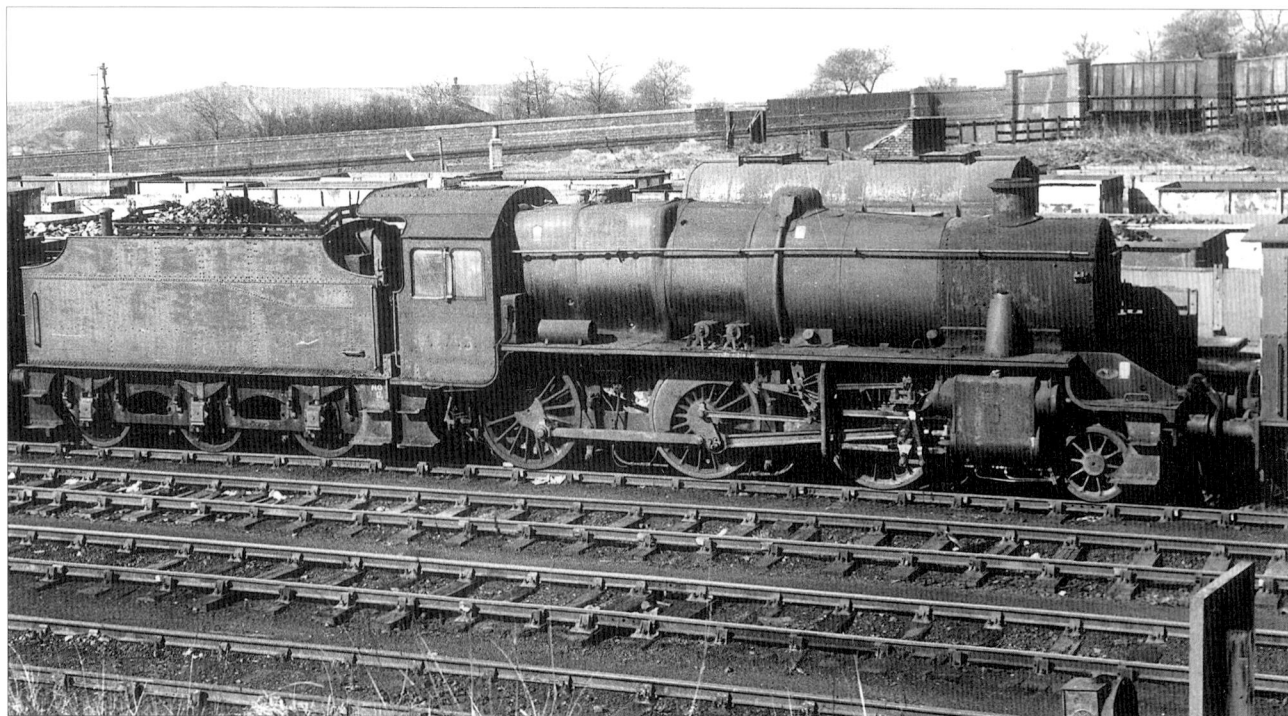

A sadly withdrawn but still-intact 42953, dumped at Springs Branch on 3 April 1966. Photograph J.L. Stevenson, courtesy Hamish Stevenson.

13254 with one of the Carlisle cranes, out on a breakdown or (more probably – the crane looks like a CCE job) a 'ballast' at Penrith, 7 June 1935. Half-cone boiler, steam issuing from the hidden GW-style safety valves. The Engine History Card shows 13254 at Kingmoor (12A) from 1 June that year, moving on to Upperby (12B) on 13 July. Even allowing for 'week ending' or 'period ending' it's hard to reconcile the record with that 12B plate on the front of the engine. But then, any book should get its readers thinking... Photograph H.C. Casserley, courtesy R.M. Casserley.

42954

Built 13/12/33 as 13254
Renumbered 2954 9/12/35
Renumbered 42954 w.e. 22/5/48

Tenders
4523 6/12/33

Repairs
9/11/35-10/12/35**LS**
25/2/37-25/3/37**LO**
7/1/38-30/4/38**HG**
24/11/39-13/1/40**HS**
24/9/42-24/10/42**LS**
1/4/44-6/5/44**HG**
4/3/46-29/3/46**LS**
7/1/47-15/2/47**LO**
24/4/48-21/5/48**HS**
25/10/49-3/12/49**HG**
16/11/51-6/12/51**LI**
27/2/53-12/3/53**LC(EO)**
19/11/53-7/1/54**LI**
18/6/54-14/8/54**HC(EO)**
8/9/54-6/10/54**LC(EO)**
28/9/55-17/11/55**HG**
30/11/57-18/1/58**HI**
2/2/60-7/3/60**NC**
18/11/60-17/2/61**HG**
9/62**'Casual'**
1/64-5/64 **Swindon**
(still there 27/9/64!)

Mileage
1933 691 (7)
1934 53,169 (18)
1935 46,534 (38)
1936 32,974 (49)
1937 27,311 (70)
1938 21,774 (134)
1939 27,965 (64)
1940 30,000 (36)
1941 35,472 (29)
1942 27,745 (62)
1943 33,640 (28)
1944 27,928 (77)
1945 29,769 (65)
1946 27,951 (103)
1947 32,032 (63)
1948 27,396 (61)
1949 24,238 (76)
1950 27,279 (21)
1951 20,178 (59)
1952 29,454 (27)
1953 23,575 (103)
1954 24,331 (105)
1955 23,231 (91)
1956 30,882 (28)
1957 24,628 (48)
1958 27,365 (43)
1959 25,477
1960 15,144
Number of weekdays out of service in brackets. Includes works attention, shed repairs/exams and 'not required'

Boilers
    6060 new
29/3/38 8405 from 2973
13/1/40 8404 from 2957
6/5/44 6057 from 2962
3/12/49 8415 from 42958
17/11/55 6057
17/2/61 6052

Sheds
Patricroft
Motherwell 8/4/34 (see 13253)
Carlisle Kingmoor 1/6/35
Carlisle Upperby 13/7/35
Birkenhead 28/12/35
Llandudno Junction 20/4/40
Bangor 26/10/40
Mold Junction 12/6/43
Llandudno Junction 19/6/43
Bangor 2/2/46 (loan)
Llandudno Junction 28/6/47
Crewe South 1/10/49
Aston 12/11/49
Crewe North 20/9/58
Nuneaton 16/9/61
Crewe South 22/6/63
Nuneaton 1/2/64
Springs Branch 5/8/64

Mileage at 12/36: 133,368
Mileage at 31/12/50: 533,868
Withdrawn w.e. 11/2/67
Cut up A. Draper, Hull

A splendid side-on (exhaust ejector 'knocking off') of 42954; the description says 'passing Peterborough (East)'. Photograph A. Scarsbrook, Initial Photographics.

1 September 1962 and the inevitable visit to Horwich for 42954 which, for our information, is stencilled CASUAL; the Engine History Card record has ended by now, remember. Among much owed to the Hughes Crabs, the Stanier moguls had the same L&Y type reverser, with a wheel as opposed to the Stanier pivoting type. The edge of the wheel can just be seen on 42954. Mixed up sand filler lids. Photograph D. Forsyth, Paul Chancellor Collection.

Off the native heath, photographs of Stanier moguls are not plentiful but 42954 (regulator blowing through) is star of the show at York shed amidst the diesels about 1963. It was a long way to go for a Nuneaton engine. Two recessed sand filler lids by now... Photograph Paul Chancellor Collection.

Returning from a London job on the Down Slow with what looks like a fitted head, 42954 runs over Bushey troughs about 1962 with a Class 'D'. It was a Nuneaton engine at the time. The mogul is not taking water, for that will be available at Brent; the Bushey troughs were really there as a last chance for engines bound for Euston (where there were no columns) to fill up. It could be an hour or more after that before they got to Camden shed. Photograph J. G. Walmsley, The Transport Treasury.

42954 after overhaul at Swindon, in 1964. The records (the Engine History Cards as we must properly term them) end with a scrawled *Maintained by Swindon 12.63* and whatever detailed records the WR then kept are not available to us. The three spare boilers did not leave Horwich, it seems, so the engines came back north with the boilers they had left with. The Swindon repairs (there were not that many of them) seem to have been lengthy affairs and 42954 was observed around the works from at least March through to late in 1964. Photograph Paul Chancellor Collection.

42955

Built 28/12/33 as 13255
Renumbered 2955 15/4/35
Renumbered 42955 w.e. 12/2/49

Tenders
4524 28/12/33

Repairs
19/2/34-11/4/34LO
28/2/35-15/4/35LS
9/6/36-24/6/36LS
31/12/36-5/3/37HG
10/5/39-24/6/39HS
17/9/41-16/10/41HG
24/6/43-31/7/43LS
2/9/44-7/10/44LO
22/1/45-10/3/45LS
28/6/46-21/9/46HG
19/1/49-10/2/49LI
2/8/50-28/8/50LI
31/8/50-1/9/50Rect
7/9/51-2/11/51HG
12/11/51-15/11/51Rect
22/3/54-24/4/54LI
25/5/54-24/6/54LC(EO)
28/5/56-13/7/56HG
4/3/58-3/4/58LI
22/1/60-2/2/60NC(EO)
9/9/60-3/11/60HI
9/63 **classification unknown**

Mileage
1934 39,113 (58)
1935 35,462 (77)
1936 40,079 (29)
1937 38,651 (90)
1938 24,585 (60)
1939 24,756 (67)
1940 27,776 (31)
1941 22,346 (74)
1942 28,368 (39)
1943 23,078 (99)
1944 24,763 (65)
1945 23,625 (68)
1946 15,841 (107)
1947 33,345 (36)
1948 26,498 (71)
1949 28,408 (58)
1950 28,300 (57)
1951 25,385 (77)
1952 31,994 (49)
1953 28,763 (50)
1954 24,880 (79)
1955 26,690 (52)
1956 22,564 (77)
1957 28,315 (64)
1958 24,256 (53)
1959 24,769
1960 21,998
Number of weekdays out of service in brackets. Includes works attention, shed repairs/exams and 'not required'

Boilers
6071 new
19/2/37 'New'*
16/10/41 8409 from 2946
21/9/46 9247 from 2947
2/11/51 6080
13/7/56 6076
was one of the three spares, 9247

Sheds
Kentish Town
Edge Hill 30/12/33
Warrington 21/9/35
Carlisle Upperby 5/3/37
Speke Junction 22/1/38
Edge Hill 29/4/39
Crewe South 10/2/40
Speke Junction 17/11/45
Edge Hill 22/6/46
Crewe South 26/4/47
Crewe North 8/1/55
Crewe South 18/4/59
Rugby 31/12/60
Nuneaton 21/1/61
Gorton 5/12/64
Heaton Mersey 12/6/65

Mileage at 12/36: 114,654
Mileage at 31/12/50: 484,994
Withdrawn w.e. 16/4/66
Cut up Birds, Long Marston

13255 in Rugby shed yard; half-cone boiler. The date is given as 18 February 1934, though the engine bears a 16 plate, the old code for Kentish Town; if the date is correct it would have been an Edge Hill loco for a month or two.

42955 resting 'out the back' at Willesden shed on 13 July 1963, fully coaled ready for its return north; that's the roundhouse, now largely serving diesels, in the right background.

As 2955 and now with the (LMS) 12B of Carlisle Upperby, where indeed the engine was photographed, 21 June 1937. It's a couple of months out of a Heavy General, and still in good external condition. Photograph H.C. Casserley, courtesy R.M. Casserley.

Dirtier by far now, at Crewe South on 7 May 1949. Photograph H.C. Casserley, courtesy R.M. Casserley.

42956

Built 19/12/33 as 13256
Renumbered 2956 30/1/35
Renumbered 42956 w.e. 29/1/49

Boilers

	6072 new
22/4/39	8403 from 2971
5/2/44	6058 from 2976
29/1/49	6052 from 2952
6/6/53	8407
1/5/58	8402

Sheds
Kentish Town
Edge Hill 13/10/34
Bletchley 23/2/35
Carlisle Upperby 20/4/35
Nuneaton 25/9/37
Birkenhead 13/11/37
Crewe South 19/9/42
Aston 26/11/60
Nuneaton 23/6/62
Stoke 22/12/62
Aintree 9/11/63
Springs Branch 25/7/64

Repairs
8/3/34-10/4/34**LO**
4/1/35-30/1/35**LS**
5/7/35-22/7/35**LO**
14/11/35-26/11/35**LS**
28/3/36-30/4/36**LS**
26/12/36**TRO**
12/12/36-20/1/37**LO**
26/8/36-4/11/37**LS**
16/3/39-22/4/39**HG**
4/2/41-8/3/41**HS**
3/4/41-17/5/41**LO**
27/12/41-16/1/42**LO**
23/12/43-5/2/44**HG**
6/2/46-9/3/46**LS**
7/2/48-17/2/48**LO**
27/7/48-29/1/49**HG**
19/1/51-13/2/51**LI**
27/4/53-6/6/53**HG**
8/8/55-10/9/55**LI**
13/11/56-12/12/56**LC(EO)**
4/3/57-30/3/57**LC**
24/2/58-1/5/58**HG**
24/12/58-9/1/59**NC(EO)**
1/12/59-16/12/59**LC(TO)**
19/2/60-8/4/60**LI**
8/62 **'Intermediate'**

Mileage
1933 575
1934 43,530 (51)
1935 37,277 (69)
1936 43,411 (60)
1937 31,718 (99)
1938 32,476 (36)
1939 23,668 (81)
1940 24,999 (44)
1941 17,552 (105)
1942 26,486 (52)
1943 27,362 (41)
1944 24,062 (63)
1945 23,553 (51)
1946 24,623 (78)
1947 23,454 (62)
1948 17,114 (171)
1949 28,487 (73)
1950 31,303 (51)
1951 28,031 (49)
1952 29,868 (65)
1953 28,669 (68)
1954 32,987 (33)
1955 26,637 (59)
1956 31,119 (63)
1957 28,716 (52)
1958 26,134 (89)
1959 27,811
1960 23,285
Number of weekdays
out of service in brackets.
Includes works attention,
shed repairs/exams and
'not required'

Tenders
4525 19/12/33
4533 3/4/36
4527 13/3/57

Mileage at 12/36: 124,793
Mileage at 31/12/50: 481,650
Withdrawn w.e. 19/9/64
Cut up Central Wagon Co, Wigan

2956 still with half-cone boiler and vacuum pump, modified top feed casing and pop safety valves on the firebox, GWR-type small ejector at the T junction of the pipe, just in front of the cab. These later gave way to the familiar LMS variety. Anti-vacuum valve on top of cylinder, beneath running plate; lubricator oil box for pony truck on inside of framing, ahead of the smokebox. Photograph J. Robertson, The Transport Treasury.

BR lined black on 42956, at Crewe South on 7 May 1949. Tender vents well within the coal space; tender riveting detail showing particularly well. Photograph H.C. Casserley, courtesy R.M. Casserley.

Now equipped with a flush riveted tender, without the attractive pattern of snaphead rivets of the originals. The change went unrecorded and the tender probably started life on an LMS 4F or a Crab. Crewe South's 42956 is under the new wires at Stockport Edgeley station, 10 September 1960. Photograph D. Forsyth, Paul Chancellor Collection.

42956 at Stoke shed in 1963. The unique ash plant beyond gives the location away. Photograph Paul Chancellor Collection.

42956 arriving with a train at Derby; this would be about 1959-60, before AWS was fitted. Photograph Norman Preedy Archive.

Aston's 42956 on the coaling ramp at Stockport Edgeley shed, 9 June 1961. This is in fact the second flush sided tender it has got in this short period – observe the preceding picture at Derby with the *second* emblem; now, later on, it has the *first* emblem... Photograph D. Forsyth, Paul Chancellor Collection.

42957

Built 23/12/33 as 13257
Renumbered 2957 29/3/35
Renumbered 42957 w.e. 12/2/49

Tenders
4526 23/12/33

Repairs
31/1/35-29/3/35LS
20/3/36-9/4/36LS
31/5/37-27/8/37HG
24/6/39-17/8/39HS
12/5/41-7/6/41LS
22/9/43-30/10/43LS
19/4/45-16/5/45HG
13/5/46-7/6/46TO
19/4/47-31/5/47HS
27/10/47-22/11/47LO
8/9/48-17/9/48LO
20/1/49-12/2/49LI
5/1/51-16/2/51HG
10/6/53-8/7/53HI
3/6/54-2/7/54LC(EO)
7/6/55-7/7/55HI
26/3/56-12/5/56HG
27/10/57-26/11/57HI
10/8/59-25/9/59LI
17/7/61-18/9/61HG
2/63 **classification unknown**

Mileage
1933 186 (3)
1934 42,237 (47)
1935 33,189 (83)
1936 35,851 (56)
1937 23,248 (112)
1938 36,941 (62)
1939 27,888 (67)
1940 30,803 (30)
1941 27,724 (52)
1942 26,619 (46)
1943 24,030 (66)
1944 28,043 (31)
1945 23,212 (80)
1946 27,616 (61)
1947 18,034 (106)
1948 29,875 (36)
1949 24,050 (48)
1950 24,140 (22)
1951 23,012 (51)
1952 25,770 (40)
1953 24,771 (50)
1954 26,474 (58)
1955 26,635 (61)
1956 26,683 (61)
1957 26,429 (49)
1958 30,155 (35)
1959 24,785
1960 28,832
*Number of weekdays
out of service in brackets.
Includes works attention,
shed repairs/exams and
'not required'*

Boilers
　　　　6073 new
18/8/37　8404 from 2972
17/8/39　6072 from 2956
16/5/45　8404 from 2954
16/2/51　6076
12/5/56　8415
18/9/61　6054

Sheds
Kentish Town
Edge Hill 13/10/34
Crewe South 20/4/47
Bletchley 13/12/47
Aston 6/3/48
Bescot 23/6/62
Bushbury 1/8/64
Oxley 17/4/65
Heaton Mersey 12/65

Mileage at 12/36: 111,463
Mileage at 31/12/50: 483,686
Withdrawn w.e. 15/1/66
Cut up T.W. Ward, Killamarsh

As 13257, in original condition at Patricroft, 24 June 1934. The coal stage pilot is 3F tank 16475 – another number series which was to be cleared in the 1934 scheme.

Edge Hill's 2957 in fine fettle. Thoroughly riveted tender with beading and cab rain strip showing well. The two Silvertown lubricators on the running plate were driven by the crank on the end of the motion link pivot. The front one fed oil to the cylinders and valves, the rear one to the coupled axleboxes. Photograph J. Robertson, The Transport Treasury.

AWS fitted, 42957 passes Chester General on the up main with the 1.20pm Llandudno-Derby, 4 August 1962. The loco had worked into Wales on the 7.47am Birmingham-Llandudno that morning. This was the great annual chance for the Stanier moguls to shine – the 4th was the Saturday of the August Bank Holiday weekend. The tender, looking perilously low on coal, is now a flush-sided one, another late change which left no mark on the Engine History Card. Photograph B.W.L. Brooksbank, Initial Photographics.

42958

Built 11/1/34 as 13258
Renumbered 2958 15/6/36
Renumbered 42958 w.e. 24/4/48

Boilers

	6074 new
25/8/37	6051 from 2945
28/7/43	8415 from 2965
2/4/49	8401 from 2950
18/3/54	6082
23/9/60	6081

Tenders
4527 11/1/34
4533 13/3/57
3969 26/8/60

Mileage
1934 35,860 (84)
1935 47,647 (34)
1936 33,912 (67)
1937 28,086(98)
1938 35,077 (47)
1939 30,910 (64)
1940 31,061 (23)
1941 26,367 (53)
1942 28,400 (35)
1943 22,168 (60)
1944 27,576 (30)
1945 24,224 (76)
1946 26,315 (22)
1947 22,343 (60)
1948 21,714 (61)
1949 24,655 (56)
1950 20,306 (33)
1951 18,729 (70)
1952 31,200 (29)
1953 24,722 (39)
1954 27,101 (82)
1955 23,890 (80)
1956 29,296 (44)
1957 24,874 (41)
1958 23,633 (62)
1959 29,606
1960 16,617
Number of weekdays
out of service in brackets.
Includes works attention,
shed repairs/exams and
'not required'

Repairs
8/3/34-3/5/34**LO**
15/5/36-15/6/36**LS**
6/10/36-14/10/36**LO**
25/6/37-2/9/37**HG**
27/7/39-6/9/39**LS**
2/4/41-29/4/41**HS**
25/6/43-28/7/43**HG**
21/8/45-15/9/45**LS**
19/4/47-17/5/47**HS**
5/3/48-24/4/48**LO**
9/3/49-2/4/49**HG**
11/4/49-27/4/49**Rect**
22/10/51-19/11/51**LI**
27/11/51-29/11/51**Rect**
31/1/53-6/2/53**LC(EO)**
16/1/54-18/3/54**HG**
3/12/55-24/1/56**LI**
1/2/58-8/3/58**LI**
26/11/59-9/12/59**NC(EO)**
4/5/60-23/9/60**HG**
4/63 **classification unknown**
5/64 **Swindon**

Sheds
Kentish Town
Crewe South 13/10/34
Carlisle Upperby 15/12/34
Edge Hill 20/6/36
Crewe South 5/7/41
Edge Hill 28/8/43
Speke Junction (loan) 9/3/46
Edge Hill 11/5/46
Crewe South 26/4/47
Nuneaton 6/12/47
Aston 17/7/48
Crewe North 20/9/58
Birkenhead 10/6/61
Nuneaton 16/6/62
Crewe South 22/6/63
Rugby 9/11/63
Gorton 2/1/65
Heaton Mersey 12/6/65

Mileage at 12/36: 117,419
Mileage at 31/12/50: 486,621
Withdrawn w.e. 20/11/65
Cut up J. Cashmore, Great Bridge

A filthy 42958, an Aston engine by now, in what nevertheless looks to be BR lined black (BRITISH RAILWAYS on the tender) rattles along about 1950, somewhere on the LNW, at a guess; the Down Slow near Tring?

42959 passing Chinley North Junction with the 11.30am Llandudno-Sheffield Midland train, inevitably a Saturday only working, on 3 September 1955. A 'dated' train, it ran from the second week in June to the second week in September. Photograph Norman Preedy.

42959

Built 4/1/34 as 13259
Renumbered 2959 22/11/34
Renumbered 42958 w.e. 6/1/51

Tenders
4528 4/1/34
4201 22/4/61

Repairs
5/12/35-28/1/36**LS**
31/3/37-14/4/37**LS**
10/6/38-17/8/38**HG**
15/11/39-23/12/39**LS**
26/5/41-5/7/41**LO**
5/11/41-22/11/41**LS**
1/12/43-26/2/44**HG**
23/2/46-6/4/46**HS**
15/10/47-27/10/47**HS**
23/12/47-14/2/48**LS**
23/5/49-25/6/49**HG**
16/2/51-15/3/51**LI**
13/10/52-20/11/52**LI**
20/10/53-20/11/53**HC**
3/8/54-3/9/54**HG**
20/3/56-10/5/56**HI**
24/6/57-2/8/57**LC**
6/9/58-10/10/58**LI**
8/11/59-16/11/59**NC(EO)**
24/1/61-14/4/61**HG**
4/62 **classification unknown**

Mileage
1934 42,885 (54)
1935 40,995 (71)
1936 35,723 (53)
1937 36,682(37)
1938 29,068 (65)
1939 31,677 (64)
1940 39,533 (21)
1941 22,224 (92)
1942 26,971 (39)
1943 18,268 (78)
1944 16,929 (91)
1945 22,075 (54)
1946 19,445 (73)
1947 17,902 (69)
1948 23,333 (77)
1949 26,881 (75)
1950 27,303 (72)
1951 27,312 (80)
1952 25,908 (80)
1953 27,066 (75)
1954 26,769 (67)
1955 29,976 (57)
1956 25,443 (76)
1957 25,944 (69)
1958 23,784 (88)
1959 32,056
1960 29,298
Number of weekdays
out of service in brackets.
Includes works attention,
shed repairs/exams and
'not required'

Boilers
       6075 new
17/8/38 6077 from 2961
26/2/44 6055 from 2964
25/6/49 6060 from 2966
3/9/54   6072
14/4/61 6057

Sheds
Kentish Town
Crewe South 13/10/34
Edge Hill 15/7/35
Nuneaton 2/5/42
Mold Junction 12/2/49
Crewe South 9/2/57
Stoke 24/11/62
Springs Branch 21/12/63

Mileage at 12/36: 119,603
Mileage at 31/12/50: 486,894
Withdrawn w.e. 25/12/65
Cut up J. Cashmore, Great Bridge

42959 at Stockport Edgeley shed on 29 April 1961, looking good despite the desultory-in-the-extreme wipe with a cloth along the tender side. This is a flush-sided one, no.4201 fitted only that week. It had previously been on Crab 42866. Photograph D. Forsyth, Paul Chancellor Collection.

42960

Built 23/12/33 as 13260
Renumbered 2960 18/4/35
Renumbered 42960 w.e. 3/12/49

Tenders
4529 23/12/33

Sheds
Kentish Town
Crewe South 13/10/34
Longsight 24/11/34
Edge Hill 9/3/35
Willesden 3/8/35
Crewe South 26/10/35
Edge Hill 8/2/36
Crewe South 7/3/36
Speke Junction 17/10/36
Edge Hill 9/1/37
Carlisle Upperby 27/2/37
Nuneaton 25/9/37
Birkenhead 13/11/37
Crewe South 19/9/42
Nuneaton 12/6/48
Aston 17/7/48
Longsight 20/1/51
Mold Junction 31/8/57
Preston 23/4/60
Nuneaton 9/9/61
Mold Junction 22/6/63
Agecroft 9/11/63
Aintree 16/11/63
Springs Branch 25/7/64
Gorton 15/5/65
Heaton Mersey 12/6/65

Mileage
1933 87 (4)
1934 41,685 (61)
1935 25,672 (119)
1936 25,041 (134)
1937 37,032 (65)
1938 28,295 (52)
1939 28,316 (70)
1940 23,035 (58)
1941 21,917 (81)
1942 20,512 (96)
1943 21,672 (77)
1944 25,327 (61)
1945 17,370 (96)
1946 30,523 (26)
1947 23,295 (83)
1948 23,352 (65)
1949 21,129 (81)
1950 24,799 (22)
1951 24,491 (80)
1952 31,073 (33)
1953 25,551 (67)
1954 22,858 (59)
1955 18,922 (104)
1956 28,481 (35)
1957 23,144 (76)
1958 24,988 (77)
1959 25,405
1960 25,704
*Number of weekdays
out of service in brackets.
Includes works attention,
shed repairs/exams and
'not required'*

Boilers
6076 new
24/9/36 'New'*
18/1/41 8405 from 2954
10/11/45 8410 from 2974
28/6/51 8404 from 2957
20/8/55 8414
*was one of the
three spares, 9246*

Repairs
23/2/34-16/4/34**LO**
28/2/35-18/4/35**LS**
12/12/35**TRO**
7/1/36**TRO**
20/7/36-12/10/36**HG**
2/1/39-15/2/39**LS**
27/12/40-18/1/41**HG**
1/3/42-4/4/42**LO**
11/8/43-28/8/43**LS**
24/6/44-27/7/44**LO**
23/3/45-21/4/45**LO**
29/9/45-10/11/45**HG**
21/1/48-21/2/48**LS**
2/11/49-3/12/49**LI**
11/5/51-28/6/51**HG**
17/4/53-23/5/53**HI**
18/5/54-23/6/54**LC(EO)**
13/7/55-20/8/55**HG**
26/11/55-30/12/55**HC**
8/3/57-18/4/57**HI**
18/4/58-28/5/58**HC(EO)**
5/12/59-22/1/60**HI**
30/6/61-13/7/61**NC(EO)**
6/62 'General'

Mileage at 12/36: 92,485
Mileage at 31/12/50: 439,059
Withdrawn w.e. 15/1/66
Cut up T.W. Ward, Killamarsh

From cobbled Bowerfold Lane, looking north towards Heaton Chapel in the summer of 1955. The new point rodding in the centre of the junction is part of the works of the modern Heaton Norris Junction signal box, newly installed. Mogul 42960 is on a Manchester London Road to Crewe local. Photograph J. Davenport, Initial Photographics.

Longsight's 42960, fresh as a daisy after overhaul at Horwich, blows off at Manchester Mayfield with the 3.20pm all stations to Crewe via Stockport, 3 September 1955. This is the same summer Saturday as when we saw 42959 earlier at Chinley North Junction – the moguls were out that day! Photograph H.C. Casserley, courtesy R.M. Casserley.

AWS fitted by now, 42960 runs through Tebay station with a northbound freight, a class D with no less than four 'fitted' wagons. Photograph Paul Chancellor Collection.

42961

Built 10/1/34 as 13261
Renumbered 2961 29/10/34
Renumbered 42961 w.e. 4/9/48

Tenders
4530 10/1/34

Sheds
Kentish Town
Crewe South 13/10/34
Longsight 24/11/34
Edge Hill 9/3/35
Aston 7/3/36
Bescot 21/11/36
Bushbury 27/3/37
Aston 3/7/37
Springs Branch 2/7/38
Shrewsbury 29/10/38
Crewe South 26/11/38
Stoke 8/7/39
Crewe South 30/9/39
Birkenhead 17/9/49
Crewe North 24/4/54
Crewe North 18/4/59
Stoke 24/11/62
Bolton 9/11/63
Aintree 23/11/63
Springs Branch 25/7/64
Gorton 15/5/65
Heaton Mersey 12/6/65

Mileage
1934 37,386 (57)
1935 34,363 (73)
1936 37,712 (53)
1937 27,384 (79)
1938 26,455 (104)
1939 35,290 (41)
1940 24,951 (63)
1941 28,360 (44)
1942 21,197 (89)
1943 27,423 (56)
1944 25,457 (83)
1945 25,395 (58)
1946 19,116 (110)
1947 24,993 (43)
1948 14,871 (166)
1949 28,794 (35)
1950 20,608 (51)
1951 21,088 (57)
1952 19,599 (66)
1953 16,940 (89)
1954 26,593 (41)
1955 24,894 (61)
1956 23,851 (81)
1957 26,521 (66)
1958 25,807 (43)
1959 22,999
1960 24,611
Number of weekdays out of service in brackets. Includes works attention, shed repairs/exams and 'not required'

Boilers
6077 new
8/6/38 8411 from 2979
27/6/42 6081 from 2977
2/9/48 8408 from 2964
19/1/54 9248
23/5/57 9247

Repairs
1/4/35-30/5/35**LS**
12/5/36-16/5/36**LO**
2/7/36-4/7/36**LO**
28/10/36-13/11/36**LS**
13/4/37-28/5/37**LO**
5/4/38-17/6/38**HG**
1/5/40-5/6/40**HS**
5/5/42-27/6/42**HG**
28/12/43-12/2/44**LS**
14/8/46-21/9/46**LS**
20/5/48-2/9/48**HG**
2/11/48-2/12/48**NC**
22/2/51-22/3/51**LI**
30/11/53-19/1/54**HG**
17/2/56-17/3/56**HI**
2/4/57-23/5/57**HG**
4/11/59-17/12/59**LI**
4/1/60-6/1/60**HC(Rect)EO**
12/62 **classification unknown**
5/64 **Swindon**

Mileage at 12/36: 109,461
Mileage at 31/12/50: 459,755
Withdrawn w.e. 21/8/65
Cut up Birds, Bynea

That fine BR (LNW) lined black on 42961, revealed to the world after General repairs before degenerating to 'overall grey'. This is the old North Staffs Derby shed site (left) on 3 June 1957 and 42961 is fresh from Horwich, working from Crewe North. The turntable served for years after the shed closed. In theory the new tender emblem should have been applied. See a similar view in the introductory notes. Photograph R.J. Buckley, Initial Photographics.

The dreaded grey is well advanced on 42961 at Stockport Edgeley station, 29 March 1960. The shed plate at the front is the 5B of Crewe South now. Photograph D. Forsyth, Paul Chancellor Collection.

42962

Built 3/1/34 as 13262
Renumbered 2962 15/12/34
Renumbered 42962 w.e. 21/8/48

Tenders
4531 3/1/34

Repairs
19/12/35-13/1/36**LS**
18/1/37-16/3/37**HG**
22/4/39-6/6/39**HS**
13/11/41-6/12/41**LS**
4/2/44-24/3/44**HG**
16/2/46-23/3/46**LS**
19/6/48-20/8/48**HS**
28/8/48-8/9/48**Rect**
4/5/50-16/6/50**HG**
21/1/52-3/3/52**HI**
10/2/53-5/3/53**LC**
9/4/53-24/4/53**LC**
21/12/54-5/2/55**HG**
27/2/57-11/4/57**LI**
9/5/59-12/6/59**HG**
6/6/61-11/7/61**LI**
1/63 **classification unknown**

Mileage
1934 44,500 (44)
1935 46,192 (53)
1936 46,527 (34)
1937 34,651 (77)
1938 28,726 (53)
1939 27,150 (64)
1940 22,811 (25)
1941 21,137 (68)
1942 30,086 (21)
1943 22,882 (42)
1944 24,432 (76)
1945 24,594 (65)
1946 24,441 (65)
1947 23,769 (52)
1948 17,284 (102)
1949 21,033 (80)
1950 19,045 (73)
1951 22,932 (37)
1952 26,980 (68)
1953 22,826 (79)
1954 24,849 (62)
1955 31,492 (65)
1956 31,309 (36)
1957 25,196 (64)
1958 28,167 (48)
1959 30,672
1960 31,815
Number of weekdays
out of service in brackets.
Includes works attention,
shed repairs/exams and
'not required'

Boilers
6078 new
2/3/37 6076 from 2960
6/6/39 6057 from 2951
24/3/44 6083 from 2983
16/6/50 6055 from 2959
5/2/55 6071
12/6/59 6053

Sheds
Leeds Holbeck
Crewe South 13/10/34
Preston 9/3/35
Carlisle Upperby 20/4/35
Warrington 9/5/36
Crewe South 21/2/42
Bangor 18/11/44
Crewe South 16/12/44
Speke junction 11/12/48
Crewe South 9/2/52
Nuneaton 30/6/62

Mileage at 12/36: 137,219
Mileage at 31/12/50: 479,260
Withdrawn w.e. 15/2/64
Cut up Crewe

The low afternoon light makes for a stirring portrait of 42962 at home on Crewe South shed, 19 August 1961. A kink in the battered old shed roads serves to emphasise the mismatch between tender and cab. Photograph D. Forsyth, Paul Chancellor Collection.

42963

Built 18/12/33 as 13263
Renumbered 2963 15/9/34
Renumbered 42963 w.e. 15/10/49

Boilers

	6079 new
30/7/37	8401 from 2969
22/8/42	8411 from 2961
10/8/46	8416 from 2967
11/1/52	6059
14/9/56	8400

Tenders
4532 18/12/33
3966 8/10/63

Mileage
1933 236 (5)
1934 44,423 (52)
1935 39,741 (84)
1936 35,798 (79)
1937 19,288 (122)
1938 30,255 (41)
1939 28,127 (80)
1940 25,409 (47)
1941 27,376 (41)
1942 26,281 (90)
1943 26,859 (37)
1944 28,519 (50)
1945 29,899 (52)
1946 23,320 (66)
1947 22,423 (95)
1948 27,709 (14)
1949 22,193 (62)
1950 23,523 (32)
1951 24,497 (55)
1952 29,342 (35)
1953 29,592 (28)
1954 28,007 (48)
1955 21,033 (106)
1956 23,526 (92)
1957 20,850 (74)
1958 25,523 (42)
1959 25,737
1960 28,107
Number of weekdays
out of service in brackets.
Includes works attention,
shed repairs/exams and
'not required'

Repairs
29/3/35-28/5/35**LS**
30/9/35-5/10/35**LO**
8/5/36-3/7/36**LS**
10/5/37-6/8/37**HG**
9/9/39-7/10/39**HS**
6/7/40-25/7/40**LO**
21/7/42-22/8/42**HG**
10/6/44-7/7/44**LS**
22/6/46-10/8/46**HG**
3/9/47-25/10/47**HS**
23/9/49-15/10/49**HI**
24/11/51-11/1/52**HG**
30/7/52-8/8/52**LC(EO)**
8/2/54-3/3/54**HI**
10/7/56-14/9/56**HG**
10/4/57-11/5/57**LC**
25/3/58-8/5/58**LI**
16/1/60-26/1/60**NC(EO)**
19/4/61-30/5/61**HI**
9/63 **classification unknown**

Sheds
Leeds Holbeck
Carlisle Upperby 13/10/34
Bescot 26/9/36
Bushbury 27/3/37
Bescot 16/10/37
Abergavenny 24/9/38
Shrewsbury 8/10/38
Crewe South 26/11/38
Bescot 19/7/43
Aston 2/10/43
Crewe North 18/9/54
Newton Heath (loan) 27/6/59
Crewe North 19/9/59
Crewe South 16/9/61
Stoke 24/11/62
Springs Branch 23/5/64

Mileage at 12/36: 120,198
Mileage at 31/12/50: 481,379
Withdrawn w.e. 16/7/66
Cut up A. Draper, Hull

42963 at Manchester London Road, 29 August 1957; Woodhead electric loco beyond. The curious covering above the box was an 'umbrella' of concrete and steel, erected during the Second World War to protect the structure from incendiary bombs. Photograph D. Forsyth, Paul Chancellor Collection.

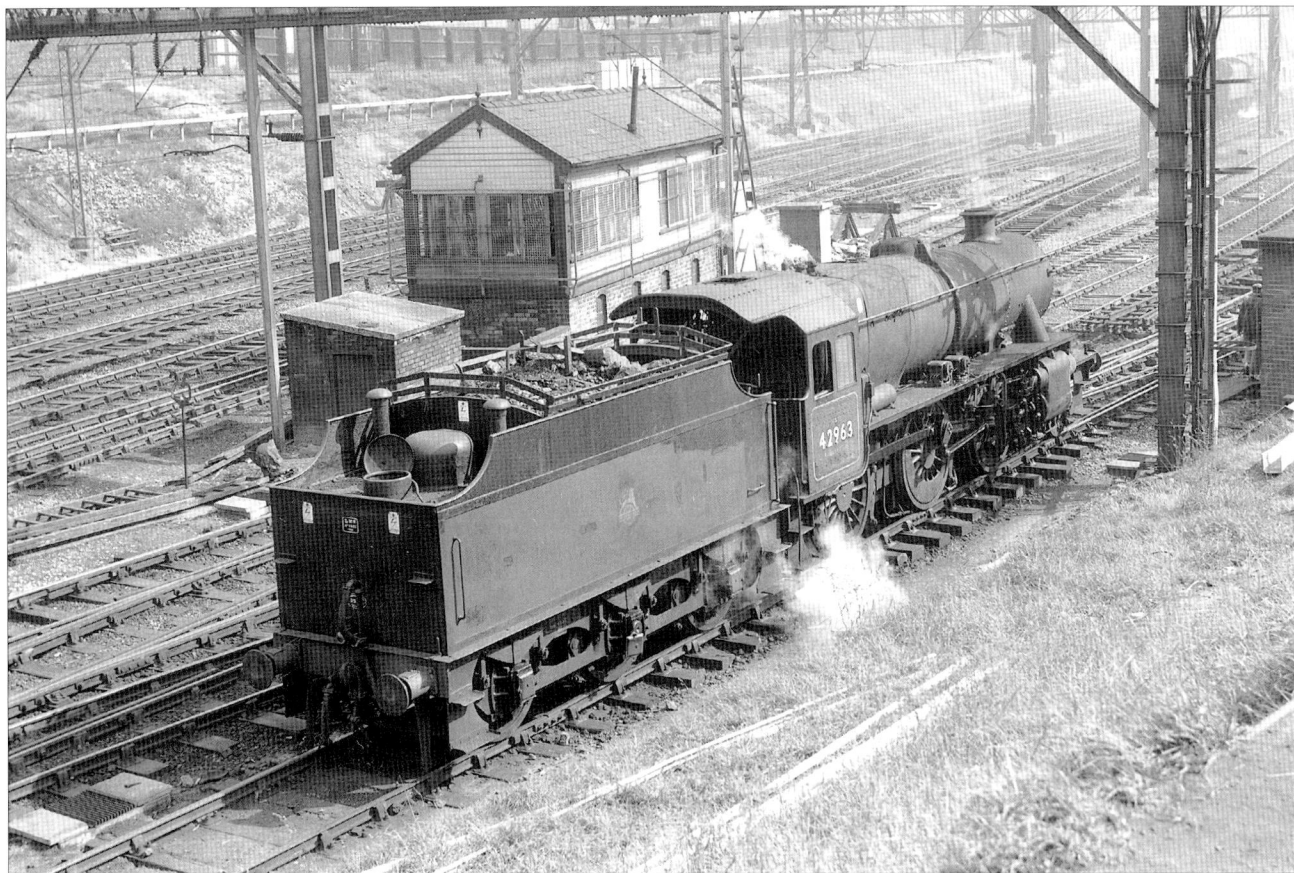

Flush-sided tender now on 42963, at Stockport Edgeley shed on 20 June 1961. This is another attachment that has gone unrecorded in the Engine History Card. This is not surprising; record keeping had largely been abandoned by now and many suitable tenders were becoming available from withdrawn engines. Horwich would rather put such a spare on than embark on a repair. Tender frames could last for ever and it was corrosion of the tank, as likely as not, that would let it down. Filler cap left open, as usual; fine view of vents and water pick-up dome. The box is Edgeley Junction No.2. Photograph D. Forsyth, Paul Chancellor Collection.

Sad, tired and withdrawn at Springs Branch, 14 July 1966. It has regained, at some point, one of the original riveted tenders. For a small class the Stanier moguls lasted intact for a considerable time and were rendered extinct only in 1966-67. So they must have had something going for them; if there was a perennial weakness, such as frame cracking, then they would have exited the BR stage quicker and sooner. Photograph C. Stacey, Initial Photographics.

42963 at Stockport Edgeley station, 29 April 1960. There was a constant to and fro of light engines between the shed and the nearby sidings. Photograph D. Forsyth, Paul Chancellor Collection.

42964

Built 8/1/34 as 13264
Renumbered 2964 11/2/36
Renumbered 42964 w.e. 8/5/48

Boilers
6080 new
22/2/38 6055 from 2949
22/1/44 8408 from 2978
7/5/48 6073 from 2981
13/7/53 6052
11/3/60 6056

Tenders
4533 8/1/34
4525 3/4/36
4179 22/6/56

Sheds
Leeds Holbeck
Carlisle Upperby 13/10/34
Warrington 9/5/36
Crewe South 27/3/37
Birkenhead 5/6/37
Edge Hill 3/7/37
Nuneaton 2/5/42
Speke Junction 15/1/49
Birkenhead 9/2/52
Crewe South 22/3/52
Birkenhead 19/9/53
Nuneaton 30/10/54
Speke Junction 8/1/55
Crewe North 14/1/56
Mold Junction 9/6/56
Crewe South 9/2/57
Aston 26/11/60
Crewe North 1/7/61
Nuneaton 16/9/61
Mold Junction 22/6/63
Birkenhead (loan) 5/10/63
Nuneaton 26/10/63
Gorton 5/12/64
Heaton Mersey 12/6/65

Mileage
1934 47,987 (18)
1935 48,683 (32)
1936 27,892 (112)
1937 34,069 (59)
1938 32,146 (77)
1939 26,146 (83)
1940 31,555 (19)
1941 27,001 (74)
1942 31,926 (63)
1943 18,443* (58)
1944 18,443* (70)
1945 22,577 (53)
1946 13,137 (96)
1947 22,630 (40)
1948 23,008 (66)
1949 21,699 (52)
1950 22,502 (55)
1951 21,547 (47)
1952 30,937 (46)
1953 24,364 (91)
1954 22,688 (57)
1955 19,423 (82)
1956 27,406 (49)
1957 25,314 (52)
1958 26,090 (95)
1959 33,406
1960 26,214
Number of weekdays out of service in brackets. Includes works attention, shed repairs/exams and 'not required'
Clerical error or statistical miracle!?

Repairs
12/12/35-11/2/36**LS**
15/10/36-28/12/36**LO**
11/12/37-3/3/38**HG**
23/10/39-6/12/39**HS**
24/10/41-12/11/41**LS**
25/8/42-3/10/42**LO**
23/12/43-22/1/44**HG**
3/9/46-12/10/46**LS**
17/3/48-9/5/48**HS**
22/5/50-24/6/50**LI**
22/11/51-15/12/51**LI**
11/5/53-13/7/53**HG**
17/3/54-14/4/54**LC**
21/9/55-2/11/55**HI**
18/6/56-11/7/56**LC**
27/9/57-26/10/57**LI**
8/9/58-16/10/58**NC(EO)**
22/10/58-23/10/58**NC(Rect)(EO)**
31/10/59-11/11/59**NC(EO)**
31/12/59-11/3/60**HG**
3/63 **classification unknown**

Mileage at 12/36: 124,562
Mileage at 31/12/50: 469,844
Withdrawn w.e. 20/11/65
Cut up J. Cashmore, Great Bridge

A fine portrait of 42964 in the BR lined black at Crewe South, with 45507 ROYAL TANK CORPS behind; D5088 was new from there in June 1960, which may indicate the place and period. Photograph Paul Chancellor Collection.

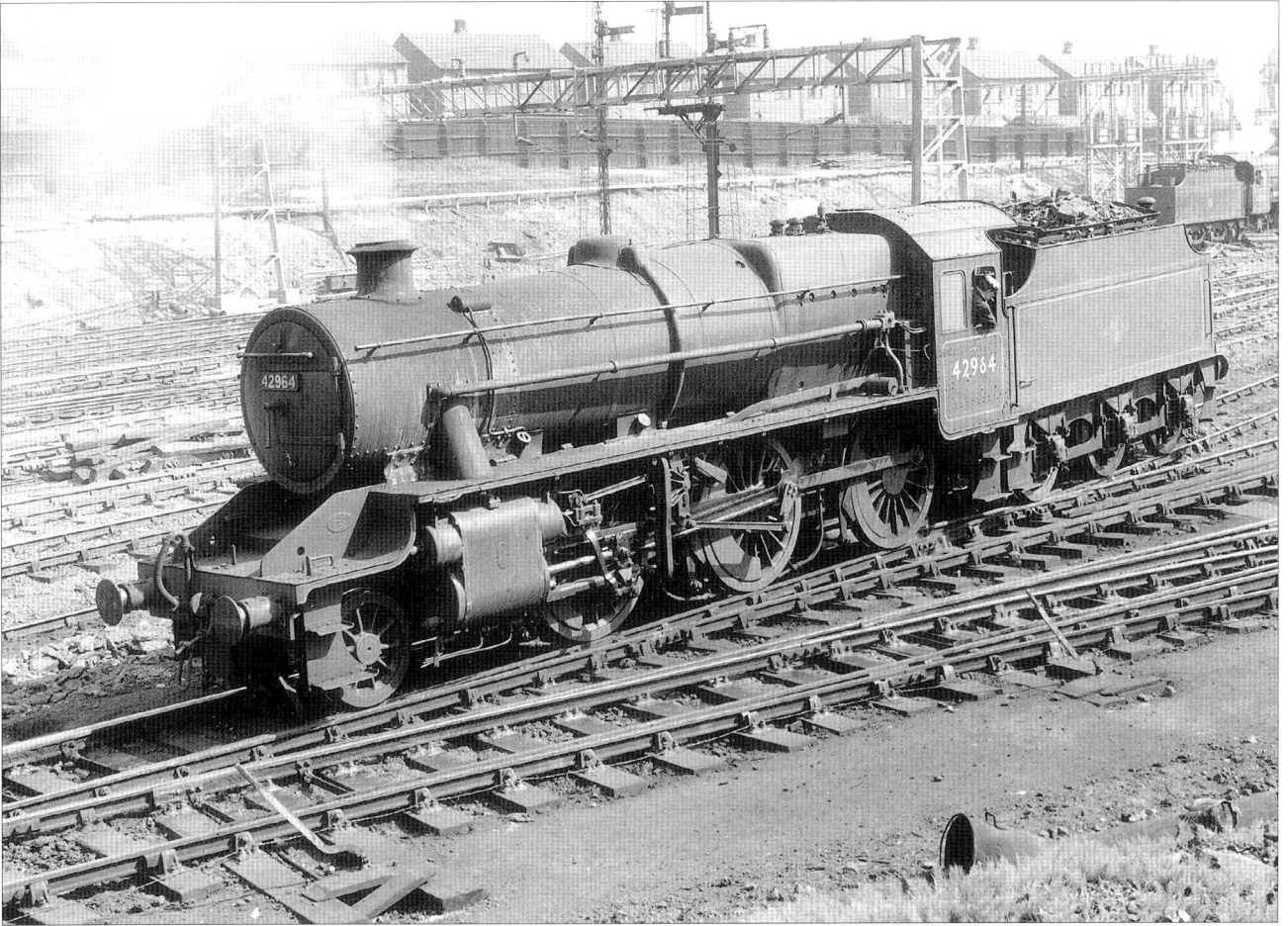

The familiar view from the Stockport Edgeley footpath again, 28 May 1960; Hughes Crab in the distance. Both have flush-sided tenders. Photograph D. Forsyth, Paul Chancellor Collection.

At Willesden shed on 16 December 1962, just a hint of that fine lined black showing through the grimy film. Photograph Peter Groom.

42965

Built 8/1/34 as 13265
Renumbered 2965 11/9/34
Renumbered 42965 w.e. 7/5/49

Boilers

	6081 new
7/12/37	8415 from 2983
7/11/42	8402 from 2980
24/12/47	9248 from 2979
14/10/53	8402
23/8/57	8405

Tenders
4534 8/1/34

Mileage
1934 37,462 (75)
1935 47,191 (30)
1936 40,302 (62)
1937 20,562 (124)
1938 36,740 (51)
1939 29,681 (70)
1940 26,494 (68)
1941 26,284 (39)
1942 16,161 (139)
1943 29,845 (43)
1944 16,833 (61)
1945 24,561 (64)
1946 27,462 (69)
1947 28,193 (82)
1948 25,637 (55)
1949 19,950 (71)
1950 23,071 (54)
1951 18,706 (66)
1952 25,077 (60)
1953 21,136 (105)
1954 30,257 (48)
1955 29,496 (65)
1956 24,903 (73)
1957 22,973 (74)
1958 28,185 (48)
1959 25,536
1960 23,252
Number of weekdays
out of service in brackets.
Includes works attention,
shed repairs/exams and
'not required'

Sheds
Leeds Holbeck
Carlisle Upperby 13/10/34
Bescot 26/9/36
Birkenhead 27/3/37
Edge Hill 3/7/37
Mold Junction 26/12/42
Llandudno Junction 5/6/48
Speke Junction 17/7/48
Birkenhead 20/10/51
Speke Junction (loan) 12/1/52
Crewe South 26/1/52
Mold Junction 14/2/53
Preston 23/4/60
Nuneaton 9/9/61
Stoke 22/12/62
Bushbury 9/3/63

Repairs
11/7/34-11/9/34**LO**
16/7/35-26/7/35**LO**
13/5/36-16/6/36**LS**
5/10/36-9/10/36**LO**
25/10/37-11/12/37**HG**
19/1/40-15/3/40**HS**
18/7/42-7/11/42**HG**
3/5/44-26/5/44**LS**
30/4/46-25/5/46**HS**
15/11/47-24/12/47**HG**
12/1/48-28/1/48**Rect**
8/4/49-5/5/49**LI**
3/5/51-29/5/51**LI**
25/11/52-18/12/52**LC(EO)**
22/8/53-14/10/53**HG**
25/8/54-11/9/54**LC(EO)**
17/4/56-17/5/56**HI**
26/6/57-23/8/57**HG**
21/9/59-27/10/59**LI**
1/8/61-15/8/61**LC(EO)**
2/62 **classification unknown**

Mileage at 12/36: 124,955
Mileage at 31/12/50: 476,429
Withdrawn w.e. 8/8/64
Cut up Cashmores, Great Bridge

First days on the Midland for 13265. Rising behind is the beer bottling plant that stood next to Kentish Town shed. The serif numbers of the smokebox plates were made from the original Johnson Midland Railway pattern! Full-cone boiler from new. No cab look-out screens, or 'cinder guards' as they are sometimes termed, at first.

Many years on, a very dilapidated 42965 awaits renaissance at Horwich. This is probably the year of its last (recorded) Heavy General, 1957. Particularly good representation of the 18 inch narrow gauge tracks. Photograph J. Davenport, Initial Photographics.

42966

Built 10/1/34 as 13266
Renumbered 2966 30/1/36
Renumbered 42966 w.e. 5/3/49

Tenders
4535 10/1/34

Repairs
7/1/36-30/1/36LS
9/10/37-20/11/37HG
20/2/40-6/4/40HS
18/7/41-9/8/41LO
18/9/42-5/12/42HG
12/3/45-29/3/45LS
22/7/47-12/9/47HS
22/9/47-26/9/47NC(Rect)
28/10/47-29/10/47NC(Rect)
10/1/49-5/3/49HG
2/2/51-3/3/51HI
17/7/52-24/7/52LC(EO)
10/8/53-24/9/53HI
6/10/53-8/10/53NC(Rect)
13/1/55-17/3/55HG
28/6/57-9/8/57LI
3/9/58-2/10/58LC
13/8/59-27/11/59HG
5/62 **classification unknown**

Mileage
1934 48,395 (25)
1935 44,394 (69)
1936 40,248 (63)
1937 36,487 (78)
1938 30,384 (68)
1939 30,483 (87)
1940 22,342 (81)
1941 26,175 (49)
1942 15,965 (136)
1943 27,643 (31)
1944 27,243 (39)
1945 29,962 (55)
1946 29,463 (36)
1947 20,319 (99)
1948 29,410 (14)
1949 21,241 (77)
1950 24,798 (33)
1951 23,549 (62)
1952 26,287 (55)
1953 22,759 (74)
1954 26,081 (54)
1955 22,313 (91)
1956 28,615 (44)
1957 28,724 (65)
1958 23,213 (75)
1959 20,290
1960 32,494
*Number of weekdays
out of service in brackets.
Includes works attention,
shed repairs/exams and
'not required'*

Boilers
6082 new
14/11/37 8414 from 2982
6/4/40 8406 from 2974
5/12/42 6060 from 2979
5/3/49 6081 from 2961
17/3/55 6075
27/11/59 8408

Sheds
Leeds Holbeck
Carlisle Upperby 13/10/34
Nuneaton 25/9/37
Crewe South 4/2/39
Stoke 8/7/39
Crewe South 30/9/39
Bescot 17/7/43
Aston 2/10/43
Willesden 5/12/53
Crewe South 8/12/56
Crewe North 3/5/58
Aston 16/9/61
Bescot 23/6/62
Bushbury 11/8/62

Mileage at 12/36: 133,037
Mileage at 31/12/50: 504,952
Withdrawn w.e. 25/7/64
Cut up J. Cashmore, Great Bridge

42966 on shed at Willesden, on 29 April 1961; with the class based in the North West (defining it broadly) the effective limits of travel were Carlisle and Willesden. Once the brief early allocation north of the border was over with they seem almost never to have penetrated into Scotland. Photograph Stephen Summerson.

42967

Built 8/1/34 as 13267
Renumbered 2967 11/12/35
Renumbered 42967 w.e. 3/7/48

Boilers

	6083 new
30/8/37	6079 from 2963
1/5/41	8416 from 2972
23/3/46	6080 from 2972
29/8/51	8411 from 42977
24/2/56	8404

Tenders
4536 8/1/34
4324 23/6/48
4515 22/3/57
4228 19/5/62
4205 11/3/63

Mileage
1934 47,111 (54)
1935 32,078 (110)
1936 36,515 (30)
1937 21,874 (94)
1938 30,662 (45)
1939 30,027 (43)
1940 22,956 (86)
1941 19,182 (106)
1942 22,413 (63)
1943 27,392 (38)
1944 23,417 (50)
1945 20,595 (72)
1946 16,797 (109)
1947 18,153 (63)
1948 18,445 (74)
1949 20,088 (42)
1950 17,862 (76)
1951 17,387 (58)
1952 22,108 (33)
1953 19,272 (72)
1954 20,085 (63)
1955 19,171 (72)
1956 22,173 (72)
1957 20,411 (81)
1958 24,896 (63)
1959 28,485
1960 22,055
Number of weekdays
out of service in brackets.
Includes works attention,
shed repairs/exams and
'not required'

Repairs
12/9/35-11/11/35**LS**
11/1/37-19/1/37**LO**
28/6/37-3/9/37**HG**
22/1/40-21/3/40**LS**
24/2/41-1/5/41**HS**
20/11/42-9/1/43**LS**
11/7/44-5/8/44**LS**
17/11/45-23/3/46**HG**
15/2/47-8/3/47**LO**
5/6/48-1/7/48**HS**
19/7/50-24/8/50**LI**
28/8/50-1/9/50**Rect**
20/7/51-29/8/51**HG**
29/12/53-30/1/54**LI**
21/1/56-24/2/56**HG**
21/3/57-12/4/57**LC**
29/3/58-30/4/58**HI**
24/4/60-17/6/60**LI**
22/6/60-23/6/60**RectNC(EO)**
4/8/61-9/8/61**NC(EO)**
2/10/61-27/10/61**LC**
3/63 **classification unknown**

Sheds
Willesden
Edge Hill 20/4/35
Warrington 7/3/36
Bescot 26/9/36
Birkenhead 27/3/37
Mold Junction 10/8/57
Chester 10/6/61
Nuneaton 16/6/62
Gorton 2/1/65
Heaton Mersey 12/6/65

Mileage at 12/36: 115,704
Mileage at 31/12/50: 425,567
Withdrawn w.e. 30/4/66
Cut up Birds, Long Marston

The glories of the BR lined black, as exhibited on 42967 at Horwich, 6 April 1963. The front numbers of the Stanier moguls were often quite different from the BR 'norm', as instanced here – compare the angular figures of the 2-6-0 with the Gill sans of 48303 alongside for instance. Photograph D. Forsyth, Paul Chancellor Collection.

Even closer glory (see previous page) of the BR lined black, on the same occasion at Horwich, 6 April 1963. Photograph D. Forsyth, Paul Chancellor Collection.

42968

Built 24/1/34 as 13268
Renumbered 2968 20/9/35
Renumbered 42968 w.e. 18/12/48

Tenders
4537 24/1/34

Sheds
Willesden
Edge Hill 20/4/35
Crewe South 13/7/35
Aston 14/12/35
Bescot 21/11/36
Birkenhead 12/6/37
Edge Hill 26/11/38
Willesden 10/5/41
Nuneaton 22/11/41
Crewe South 21/2/42
Crewe North 3/5/58
Birkenhead 10/6/61
Nuneaton 16/6/62
Mold Junction 22/6/63
Springs Branch 23/5/64
Gorton 15/5/65
Heaton Mersey 12/6/65
Springs Branch 1/66

Mileage
1934 41,087 (61)
1935 26,809 (110)
1936 36,729 (56)
1937 24,837 (78)
1938 28,180 (58)
1939 28,279 (85)
1940 33,155 (16)
1941 29,508 (65)
1942 28,388 (38)
1943 19,511 (71)
1944 21,370 (104)
1945 19,242 (47)
1946 23,381 (94)
1947 9,763 (206)
1948 18,179 (107)
1949 27,287 (58)
1950 29,894 (48)
1951 30,357 (48)
1952 24,185 (87)
1953 27,700 (74)
1954 30,879 (43)
1955 25,780 (63)
1956 24,272 (100)
1957 23,285 (81)
1958 28,821 (44)
1959 26,850
1960 25,833
Number of weekdays
out of service in brackets.
Includes works attention,
shed repairs/exams and
'not required'

Boilers
	8400 new
29/9/37	6074 from 2958
11/3/44	8403 from 2956
7/11/47	6082 from 2970
29/9/53	6073
26/9/57	8412

Repairs
22/7/35-20/9/35**LS**
22/10/36-2/12/36**LS**
14/8/37-7/10/37**HG**
27/10/39-13/12/39**HS**
30/10/41-15/11/41**LS**
21/1/44-11/3/44**HG**
29/8/46-4/10/46**LS**
24/4/47-7/11/47**HO**
13/11/47-17/11/47**Rect**
28/10/48-18/12/48**LS**
30/12/48-5/1/49**Rect**
11/6/49-24/6/49**HC**
18/4/51-16/5/51**LI**
14/8/52-26/9/52**LC(EO)**
18/8/53-29/9/53**HG**
25/5/56-3/7/56**LI**
12/8/57-25/9/57**HG**
10/12/59-19/1/60**LI**
11/62 **'Intermediate'**

Mileage at 12/36: 104,625
Mileage at 31/12/50: 445,599
Withdrawn w.e. 31/12/66
PRESERVED

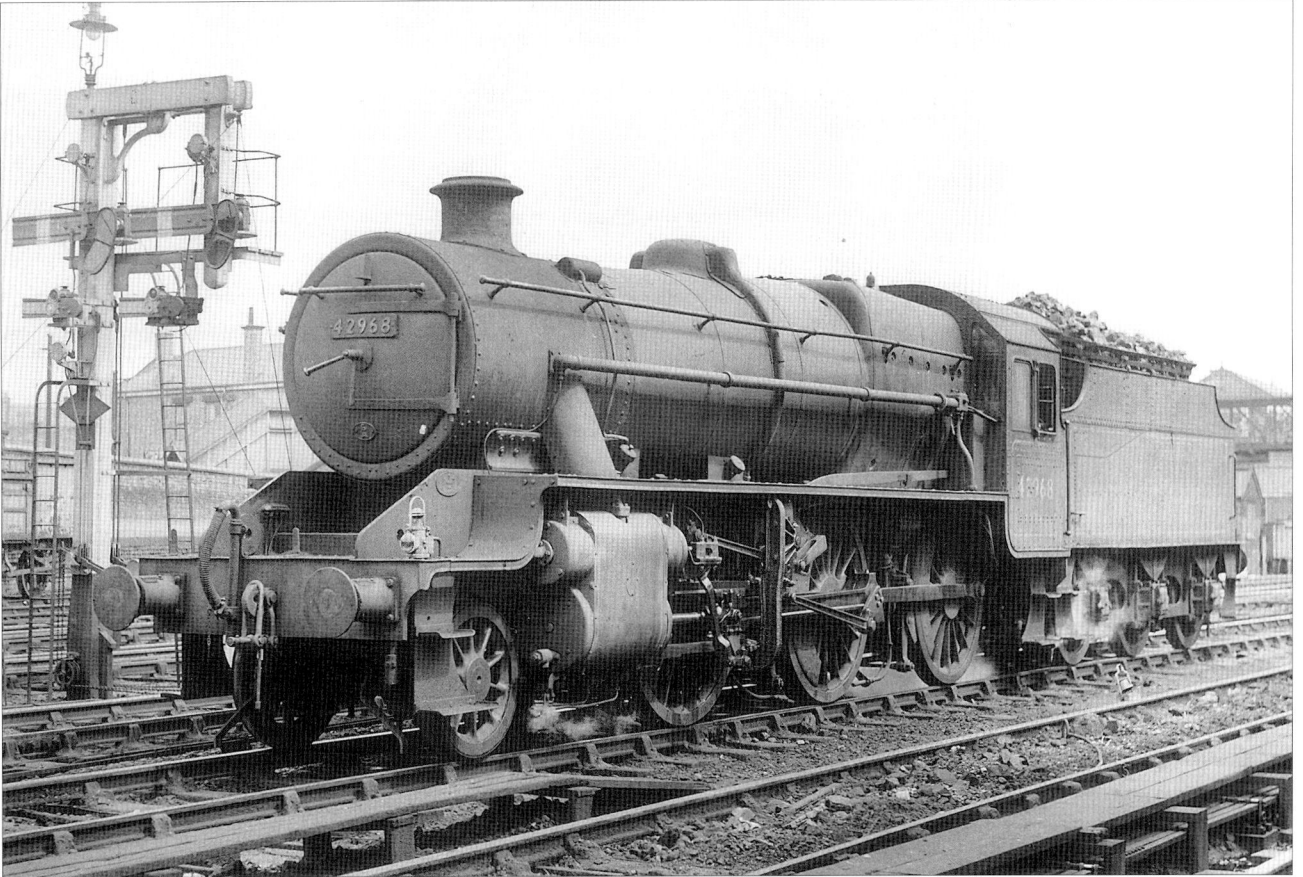

42968, BR lined black, riveted tender, at Chester it is said, in 1959. Oddly the works plate is higher than usual on this engine. Explain that one! She is now the preserved joy of the Stanier Mogul Fund and the plate is still in the same position.

The now-preserved 42968 (aptly termed 'The Mighty Mogul') visits Edgeley and once again makes for a fine portrait from the footpath to the shed (just off to the right) in this case on 15 March 1961. And there's that plate again... This particular one was a bit unlucky compared to most and over 1946-48 (a period of relatively poor mileages for many engines it must be said, due to traffic conditions, weather, labour shortage, wartime neglect and so on) contrived to spend some 400 days out of service – well over a year). A platelayer is taking the opportunity to get some water from the exhaust injector overflow. Photograph D. Forsyth, Paul Chancellor Collection.

42968 at Preston, on a very late passenger working (according to the lamp code – the 'top' lamp now lowered to the smokebox waist) in September 1966. The clean condition is owed to its work on the Wigan Area Brake Van tour, 13 August 1966. There was one other Stanier mogul left at the end and the Fund's notes recall that both, 42954 and 42968, were in Preston station within half an hour of each other on 14 December 1966. The former was on a soda ash train, and the Fund's 42968 on a parcels from Lime Street. Photograph A.G. Forsyth, Initial Photographics.

As nature intended... now with Stanier 4,000 gallon tender, ex-Black Five 45110, fitted at the end of 1994. Here she is on the Severn Valley Railway, 30 April 1995. In 1970, a few Stanier 8F Society members had taken a break from 8233 and trekked to Woodham Bros. scrap yard in Barry to gaze upon the last survivor of Sir William Stanier's first design, mogul 42968. The four decided that very evening that such a historic engine could not be abandoned to her fate, and the Stanier Mogul Fund was formed to ensure her preservation. There then followed the usual pattern of fund raising and yard visits to prepare her for salvation on the Severn Valley Railway. The purchase price of £3,575 was handed over on 1 September 1973 and 42968 was towed from Barry to Bewdley *dead on her own wheels* over the night of 13-14 December 1973, just avoiding an ASLEF strike! Photograph R. Greaves, courtesy Stanier Mogul Fund.

42969

Built 12/1/34 as 13269
Renumbered 2969 21/8/35
Renumbered 42969 w.e. 24/9/49

Tenders
4538 12/1/34
4201 26/5/55
4528 22/4/61

Repairs
22/5/34-21/6/34**LO**
5/7/35-21/8/35**LS**
15/9/36-18/9/36**LO**
7/4/37-17/6/37**HG**
28/4/39-27/5/39**LS**
21/4/41-31/5/41**LO**
11/10/41-25/10/41**HS**
29/1/43-20/3/43**HG**
27/2/45-17/3/45**LS**
11/11/46-8/2/47**HS**
25/8/49-22/9/49**LI**
18/8/50-31/8/50**LC**
7/3/51-19/4/51**LI**
5/1/53-10/2/53**HG**
6/7/53-7/8/53**LC(TO)**
31/10/53-27/11/53**LC(TO)**
24/5/55-8/7/55**HI**
7/2/57-15/3/57**LI**
8/9/58-31/10/58**HG**
8/2/61-10/4/61**HI**
13/11/61-22/11/61**NC(EO)**

Mileage
1934 38,401 (56)
1935 25,369 (106)
1936 37,716 (46)
1937 25,117 (100)
1938 24,839 (50)
1939 24,004 (57)
1940 22,212 (78)
1941 20,089 (96)
1942 26,121 (47)
1943 23,306 (75)
1944 23,855 (41)
1945 23,194 (46)
1946 17,470 (73)
1947 18,655 (76)
1948 20,871 (37)
1949 20,456 (64)
1950 20,839 (45)
1951 16,973 (81)
1952 22,288 (34)
1953 19,648 (109)
1954 20,188 (60)
1955 21,855 (67)
1956 25,610 (50)
1957 23,372 (66)
1958 19,886
1959 28,353
1960 24,863
Number of weekdays
out of service in brackets.
Includes works attention,
shed repairs/exams and
'not required'

Boilers
8401 new
9/6/37   6071 from 2955
20/3/43 8413 from 2971
8/2/47   8407 from 2973
10/2/53 6053
31/10/58 6073

Sheds
Rugby
Willesden 27/1/34
Warrington 20/10/34
Crewe South 20/4/35
Aston 30/11/35
Willesden 14/11/36
Bushbury 27/3/37
Birkenhead 17/2/40
Nuneaton 16/6/62
Crewe South 22/6/63
Rugby 9/11/63
Crewe South 14/11/64

Mileage at 12/36: 101,486
Mileage at 31/12/50: 411,514
Withdrawn w.e. 14/11/64
Cut up T.W. Ward, Killamarsh

42969 at Birkenhead shed, 5 April 1953. The moguls were frequently allocated here and 42969 was one at the time, but you'll struggle to find pictures of them in the area. A WR Grange 4-6-0 stands alongside.

Having declared how difficult it is to find pictures of them in the area, here's another one! Across the platform ends to 42969 on a train at Hooton, 2 June 1961. Photograph H.C. Casserley, courtesy R.M. Casserley.

Still a Birkenhead engine, 42969 at Horwich on 8 April 1961. She has the Crab tender 4201, our old friend from 42959 and reverted to a riveted one after this – you have to allow a few days either way in the dates. Photograph D. Forsyth, Paul Chancellor Collection.

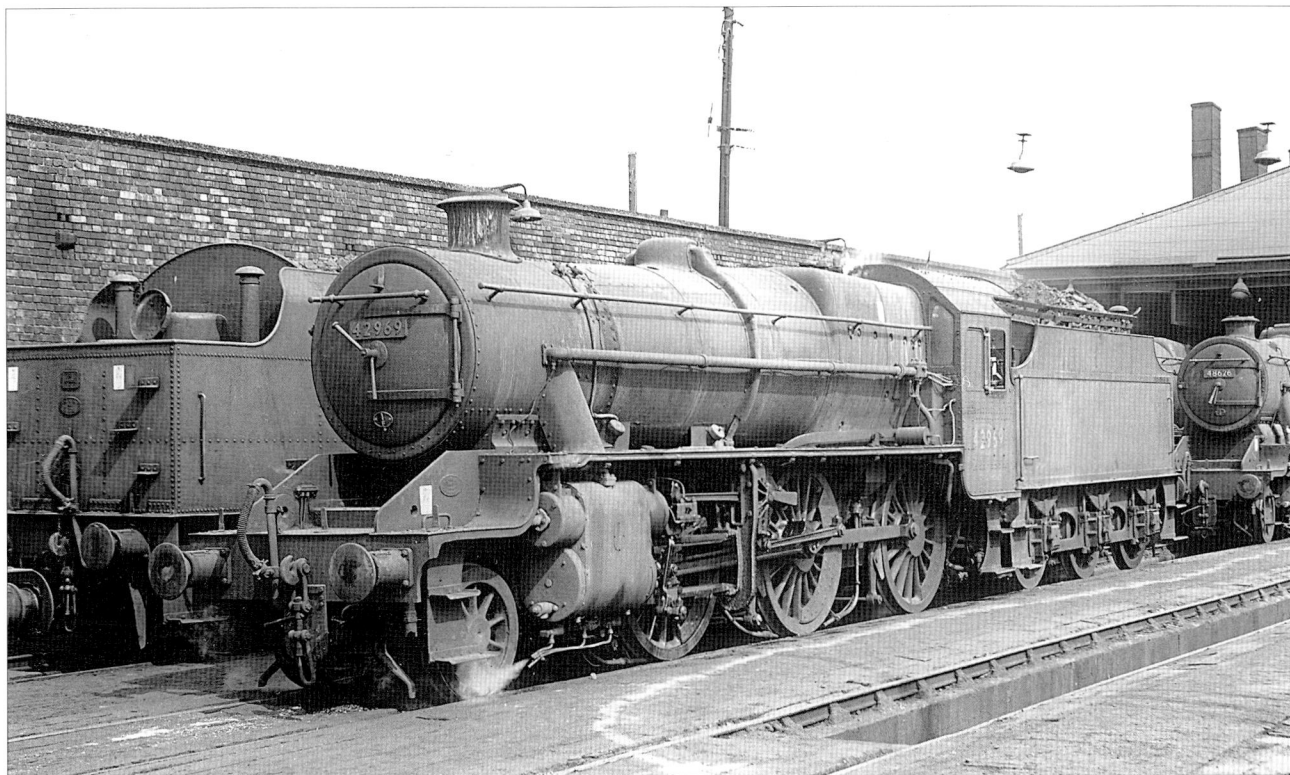

At Willesden shed, regulator blowing through, 6 July 1964. As for that whitish trail – has someone just gone by with a leaking barrow of sand? Photograph Peter Groom.

42970

Built 11/1/34 as 13270
Renumbered 2970 13/6/35
Renumbered 42970 w.e. 16/12/50

Boilers

	8402 new
6/4/38	6052 from 2946
22/5/43	6082 from 2953
5/9/47	6056 from 2980
24/1/53	8413
19/10/57	9248

Tenders
4539 11/1/34

Mileage
1934 34,734 (90)
1935 30,541 (92)
1936 34,069 (60)
1937 31,238 (107)
1938 22,583 (87)
1939 25,249 (48)
1940 23,435 (70)
1941 25,277 (56)
1942 23,090 (51)
1943 22,104 (73)
1944 22,359 (68)
1945 28,508 (58)
1946 21,608 (52)
1947 15,897 (135)
1948 21,117 (43)
1949 21,031 (43)
1950 18,007 (75)
1951 17,612 (69)
1952 17,054 (64)
1953 22,862 (72)
1954 19,664 (82)
1955 21,539 (88)
1956 23,415 (45)
1957 19,915 (78)
1958 24,845 (69)
1959 26,229
1960 19,670
Number of weekdays out of service in brackets. Includes works attention, shed repairs/exams and 'not required'

Sheds
Aston 20/1/34
Willesden 27/1/34
Edge Hill 20/10/34
Crewe South 15/6/35
Birkenhead 9/5/36
Carlisle Upperby 9/10/36
Birkenhead 19/6/37
Barrow 3/7/37
Stockport Edgeley 25/9/37
Bushbury 2/10/37
Birkenhead 17/2/40
Newton Heath 4/7/59*
Birkenhead 12/9/59
Nuneaton 16/6/62
Mold Junction 22/6/63
Birkenhead 5/10/63
Nuneaton 26/10/63
loan, probably

Repairs
7/5/34-30/6/34**HO**
25/4/35-13/6/35**LS**
7/9/36-9/10/36**LS**
8/2/37-5/5/37**LO**
11/2/38-21/4/38**HG**
15/6/40-3/7/40**LS**
12/4/43-22/5/43**HG**
9/9/44-14/10/44**LS**
8/5/45-9/6/45**LO**
6/5/47-5/9/47**HS**
18/2/50-10/3/50**LI**
6/12/50-6/1/51**HC**
9/12/52-24/1/53**HG**
18/3/54-22/4/54**LC(EO)**
24/3/55-14/5/55**HI**
22/8/57-19/10/57**HG**
25/5/60-14/7/60**HI**
25/7/60-18/8/60**NC(EO)**
4/9/61-15/9/61**NC(EO)**
6/62 **'Intermediate'**

Mileage at 12/36: 99,344
Mileage at 31/12/50: 420,847
Withdrawn w.e. 24/10/64
Cut up J. Cashmore, Great Bridge

As good a portrait as you'll find – the taper tale of things to come. And observe how modern and 'new' 13270 looks compared to the line-up behind. It was slightly odd that Stanier's reign should be marked at first by a 2-6-0; only in Britain was the type not regarded as verging on the obsolescent and it was even odder that BR perpetuated the wheel arrangement well into the 1950s. Maybe it was the country's long reliance on the 0-6-0, of which the 2-6-0 was, in essence, merely a development.

Those Johnson numerals stand out well at Willesden, 22 April 1934. The old code of 2 denotes its home shed, Willesden.

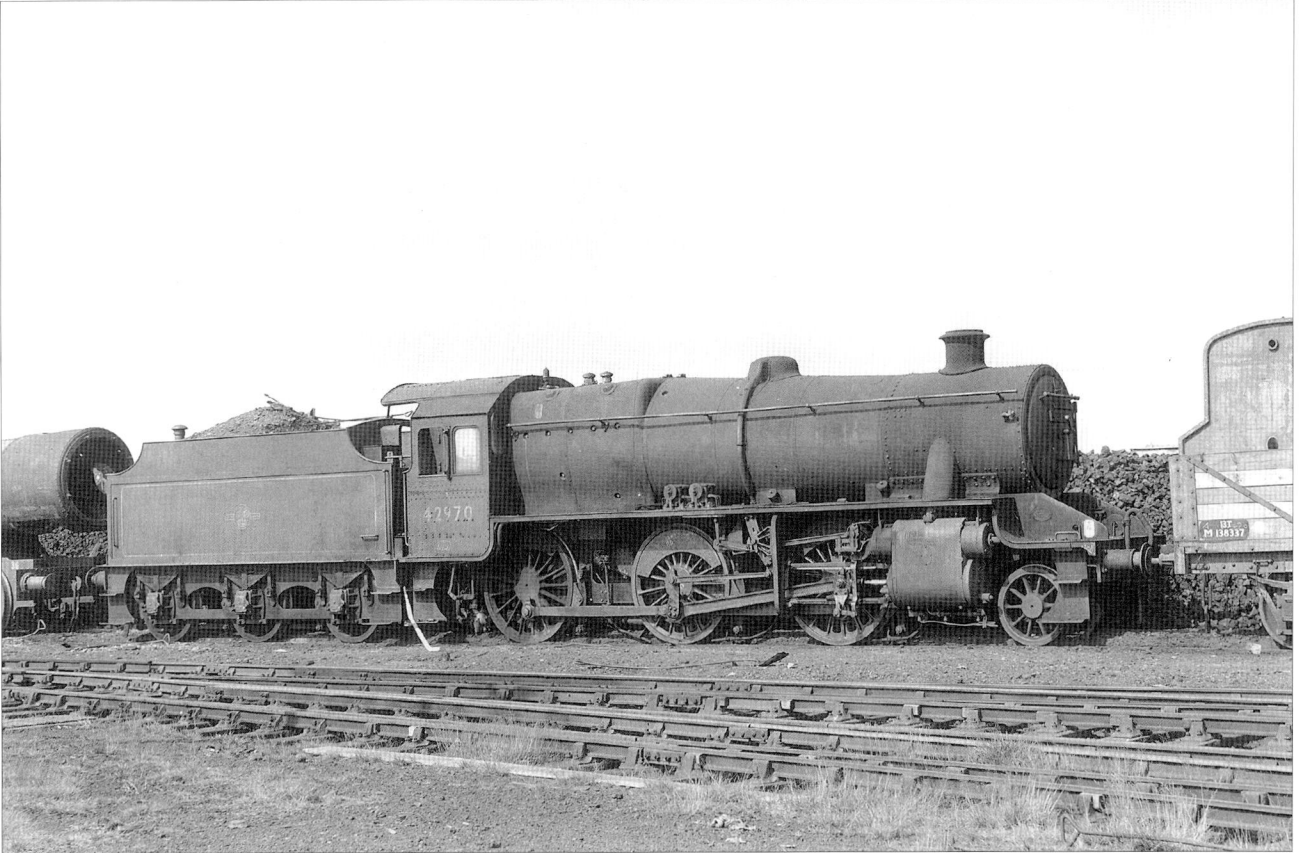

Horwich Works yard, and on 2 September 1961 a weary 42970 has made it there over the Mersey from Birkenhead for a Non Classified repair. This normally meant an engine had suffered some failure or needed a repair beyond the capabilities of the shed. By some accounts the Stanier moguls were prone to breakdown, more so than the Crabs, though mileages seemed little different between the two types. At Crewe the failure to empty the (by now flush-sided) tender preparatory to entering the works would have caused a major incident! Perhaps the tender was destined to stay outside for the duration of the repair. The curious item in the wagon on the right is a fuel tank off a 350hp diesel shunter. Photograph D. Forsyth, Paul Chancellor Collection.

In a familiar picture a Gorton Crab, 42878, has made it down to Gloucester on 28 December 1963. It makes for an interesting comparison with Nuneaton's 42970 at the old Midland Barnwood shed; breakdown train behind. Photograph Norman Preedy.

42971

Built 10/1/34 as 13271
Renumbered 2971 9/12/35
Renumbered 42971 w.e. 17/12/49

Boilers

8403	new
8/9/38	8413 from 2981
6/2/43	8406 from 2966
29/11/47	6054 from 2984
8/5/53	8409
19/12/57	8413

Tenders
4540 10/1/34
4256 12/12/57

Mileage
1934 40,244 (39)
1935 30,044 (95)
1936 37,756 (35)
1937 36,034 (48)
1938 28,196 (127)
1939 38,507 (52)
1940 25,236 (67)
1941 25,289 (68)
1942 19,347 (93)
1943 22,588 (63)
1944 20,630 (33)
1945 20,959 (73)
1946 25,151 (41)
1947 22,199 (117)
1948 36,073 (41)
1949 25,583 (47)
1950 23,921 (57)
1951 20,546 (45)
1952 23,337 (90)
1953 26,184 (98)
1954 27,961 (67)
1955 21,765 (97)
1956 28,724 (55)
1957 23,252 (78)
1958 27,747 (62)
1959 33,400
1960 24,766

*Number of weekdays
out of service in brackets.
Includes works attention,
shed repairs/exams and
'not required'*

Repairs
24/10/35-9/12/35LS
3/8/36-8/8/36LO
14/4/37-27/4/37LS
29/6/38-8/9/38HG
22/4/40-27/5/40HS
2/11/42-6/2/43HG
12/5/43-15/5/43LO
11/5/45-23/6/45LS
24/12/46-1/2/47LS
20/9/47-29/11/47HG
26/11/49-17/12/49HI
12/12/50-20/1/51LI
10/3/53-8/5/53HG
23/5/54-17/6/54LC(EO)
11/4/55-13/5/55LI
28/5/56-20/6/56LC(EO)
7/11/57-19/12/57HG
25/1/60-17/3/60HI
28/8/61-13/9/61LC(EO)
11/62 **classification unknown**

Sheds
Edge Hill
Willesden 27/1/34
Carstairs 8/4/34
'Patricroft' (no date)
Crewe South 1/6/35
Warrington 3/10/36
Chester 25/9/37
Birkenhead 25/11/39
Llandudno Junction 12/10/46
Speke Junction 1/10/49
Mold Junction 9/2/52
Chester 10/6/61
Birkenhead 14/10/61
Nuneaton 16/6/62
Crewe South 22/6/63
Nuneaton 9/11/63

Mileage at 12/36: 108,047
Mileage at 31/12/50: 477,760
Withdrawn w.e. 19/12/64
Cut up Cashmores, Great Bridge

42971 with what looks like Gresley stock (thrown into the fray for a summer Saturday service, the 11.30am Llandudno-Sheffield Midland) at Cheadle Heath station on 10 September 1960. The engines had a reputation in some quarters for poor, or at least erratic steaming, especially in comparison to the Hughes Crabs. Some individual performances bordering on the spectacular and repeated experience in preservation suggests nothing overly wrong but one problem would have been familiarity. A crew might get them only occasionally compared to a Crab; they were outnumbered about 6 to 1 after all and by the time the Stanier ones really became concentrated at some sheds their mechanical needs were, like other classes, increasingly neglected – more so than most, possibly. Photograph D. Forsyth, Paul Chancellor Collection.

42972

Built 15/1/34 as 13272
Renumbered 2972 5/2/36
Renumbered 42972 w.e. 9/4/49

Tenders
4541 15/1/34

Repairs
7/1/36-5/2/36**LS**
31/10/36-5/11/36**LO**
21/5/37-17/8/37**HG**
30/8/39-7/10/39**LS**
22/2/41-29/3/41**HS**
27/5/43-19/6/43**LS**
21/12/43-27/12/43**LO**
19/3/45-25/4/45**HG**
4/3/48-3/4/48**HS**
19/4/48-23/6/48**TRO**
25/6/48-25/6/48**NCRect**
28/3/49-8/4/49**LC**
29/7/49-27/8/49**HC**
15/5/50-17/6/50**HG**
16/5/52-14/6/52**LI**
24/6/52-12/7/52**Rect**
15/10/53-11/11/53**LC**
12/11/54-18/12/54**HG**
15/2/56-10/3/56**LC**
14/3/57-18/4/57**LI**
2/9/59-23/10/59**LI**

Mileage
1934 41,107 (43)
1935 41,091 (50)
1936 37,988 (51)
1937 27,425 (88)
1938 32,678 (64)
1939 21,857 (75)
1940 19,057 (77)
1941 20,768 (84)
1942 27,618 (38)
1943 27,115 (57)
1944 27,359 (36)
1945 23,500 (75)
1946 20,922 (23)
1947 24,456 (57)
1948 15,292 (133)
1949 24,048 (76)
1950 27,114 (56)
1951 30,384 (40)
1952 28,767 (65)
1953 25,241 (82)
1954 25,554 (76)
1955 32,791 (36)
1956 31,485 (62)
1957 27,018 (64)
1958 31,042 (48)
1959 22,706
1960 27,531
Number of weekdays
out of service in brackets.
Includes works attention,
shed repairs/exams and
'not required'

Boilers
       8404 new
4/8/37   8416 from 2984
29/3/41   6080 from 2973
25/4/45   6076 from 2975
17/6/50   6074 from 42975
18/12/54 6060

Sheds
Willesden
Carstairs 8/4/34
Motherwell (loan) 27/4/35
Preston 6/7/35
Aston 16/11/35
Warrington 21/11/36
Crewe South 21/2/42
Edge Hill 28/8/43
Speke Junction 27/10/45
Edge Hill 22/6/46
Speke Junction 20/7/46
Crewe South 24/4/48
Stoke 24/11/62
Bescot 9/3/63
Gorton 2/1/65

Mileage at 12/36: 120,186
Mileage at 31/12/50: 459,395
Withdrawn w.e. 17/4/65
Cut up R.S. Hayes, Bridgend

42972 at Crewe South shed on 18 August 1962; AWS and that style of smokebox plate numbering again. Photograph D. Forsyth, Paul Chancellor Collection.

42972, a Bescot engine when it was still in the 21 District; it was reorganised towards the end of 1963 with the West Midlands WR sheds, headed by Tyseley. The mogul, looking sprightly it must be said, is on the Up Slow at Bushey troughs with Presflos and other wagons in May 1963. Note the curious smokebox plate lettering again, which appeared on other classes too. The photographer would have been prudent to take a few steps back as the engine went by. Half a ton of water with stray coal lumps could have unpleasant consequences though, to be fair, 42972 is not actually picking up here. The combined Bakerloo and Watford DC Electric lines are over on the far side, the down line running under that extra arch in the Oxhey Road bridge, fashioned for the DC widening in 1913. Photograph J.G. Walmsley, The Transport Treasury.

42972 at Stockport Edgeley shed, 15 August 1961; buckled front running plate again. The curious wire mesh on the signal box windows (the same No.2 box is seen elsewhere in these pictures) was put up because the overhead wires were believed to be a bit close for comfort. No one wanted a signalman leaning out and electrocuting himself. Photograph D. Forsyth, Paul Chancellor Collection.

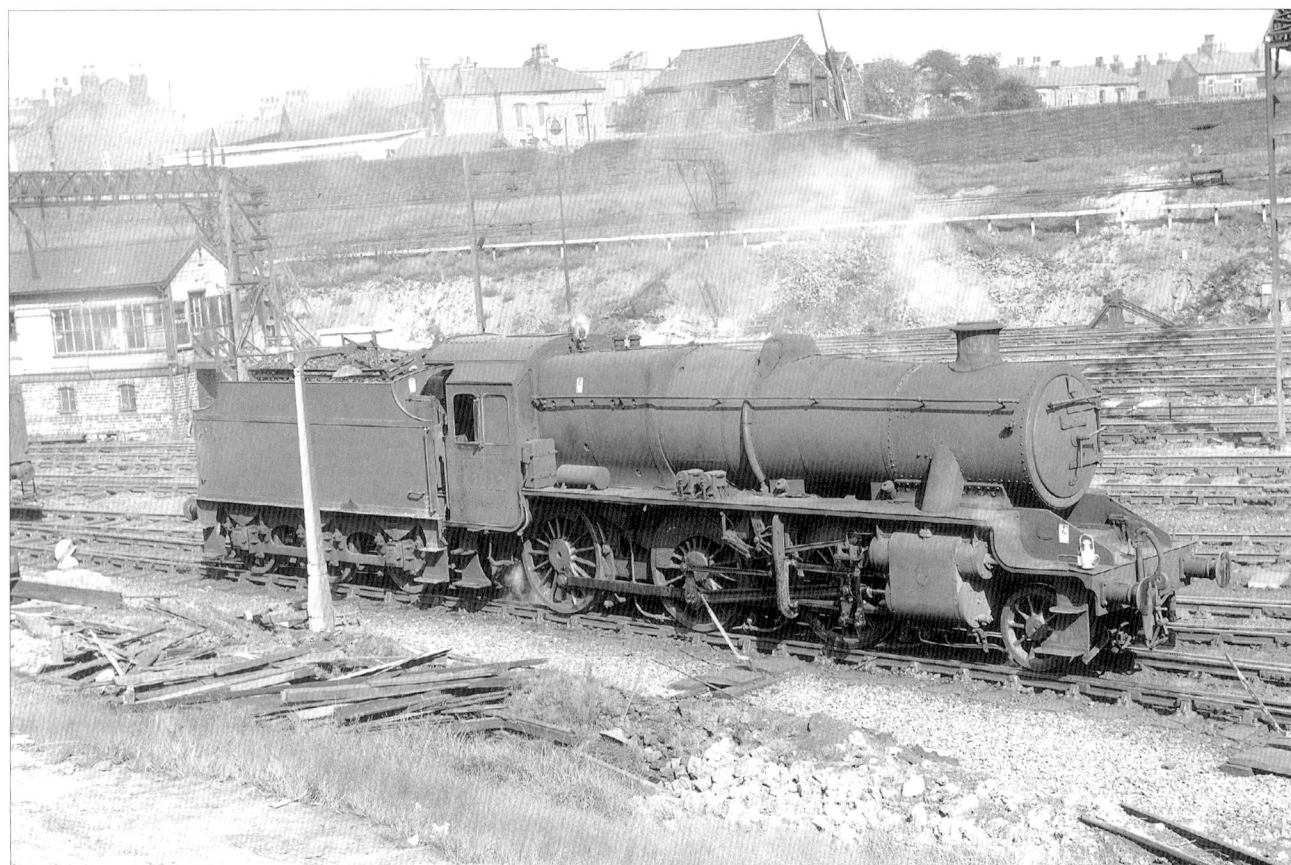

42973

Built 20/1/34 as 13273
Renumbered 2973 11/4/36
Renumbered 42973 w.e. 19/6/48

Tenders
4542 20/1/34

Sheds
Willesden
Motherwell 8/4/34
Polmadie 9/7/34
Preston 15/6/35
Aston 16/11/35
Monument Lane 21/11/36
Aston 20/3/37
Monument Lane 12/6/37
Bescot 25/9/37
Aston 28/1/39
Nuneaton 29/4/39
Speke Junction 15/1/49
Aston 27/8/49
Birkenhead 30/9/50
Mold Junction 20/6/53
Birkenhead 6/2/60
Nuneaton 16/6/62

Mileage
1934 46,162 (18)
1935 44,687 (13)
1936 35,484 (64)
1937 32,688 (57)
1938 22,856 (83)
1939 32,762 (65)
1940 21,423 (77)
1941 24,482 (48)
1942 24,457 (57)
1943 22,203 (53)
1944 19,547 (90)
1945 22,426 (44)
1946 17,850 (119)
1947 21,588 (59)
1948 20,682 (51)
1949 21,344 (55)
1950 19,365 (59)
1951 22,878 (46)
1952 23,254 (51)
1953 28,706 (46)
1954 28,149 (73)
1955 29,219 (60)
1956 25,483 (72)
1957 28,703 (33)
1958 25,596 (72)
1959 29,047
1960 19,801
Number of weekdays out of service in brackets. Includes works attention, shed repairs/exams and 'not required'

Boilers
8405 new
7/3/38 6080 from 2964
4/5/40 8407 from 2975
27/4/46 9246 from 2948
31/10/50 6078 from 2974
30/10/56 8416

Repairs
3/3/36-8/4/36LS
18/8/36-22/8/36LO
9/9/37-25/9/37LO
7/1/38-12/3/38HG
14/3/40-4/5/40HS
31/3/42-25/4/42LS
23/3/44-15/4/44LS
23/9/44-21/10/44LO
25/12/45-27/4/46HG
22/5/48-19/6/48HS
26/9/50-31/10/50HG
7/6/52-10/7/52LI
16/8/54-14/9/54LI
6/10/54-7/10/54NC(EO)Rect
24/9/56-30/10/56HG
22/11/58-30/12/58LI
19/12/60-16/2/61LI
2/10/61-11/10/61NC(EO)

Mileage at 12/36: 126,333
Mileage at 31/12/50: 450,006
Withdrawn w.e. 9/11/63
Cut up Horwich

How the mighty moguls could/should have looked! 42973 (no date available but the year is possibly 1950) by chance 'parked' next to a Stanier tender after release from the Paint Shop at Horwich. Photograph J. Davenport, Initial Photographics.

79

42974

Built 16/1/34 as 13274
Renumbered 2974 25/2/36
Renumbered 42974 w.e. 1/7/50

Tenders
4543 16/1/34

Sheds
Willesden
Motherwell 8/4/34
Polmadie 9/7/34
Preston 13/7/35
Warrington 16/11/35
Springs Branch 13/11/37
Birkenhead 5/3/38
Nuneaton 10/5/41
Crewe South 21/2/42
Speke Junction 17/11/45
Crewe South 24/4/48
Nuneaton 19/6/48
Aston 17/7/48
Bescot 23/6/62
Gorton 2/1/65
Heaton Mersey 12/6/65

Mileage
1934 49,962 (19)
1935 41,157 (47)
1936 28,186 (73)
1937 23,845 (72)
1938 24,045 (74)
1939 19,477 (98)
1940 23,843 (61)
1941 24,246 (53)
1942 28,232 (35)
1943 24,016 (86)
1944 25,936 (56)
1945 21,708 (81)
1946 19,589 (37)
1947 23,775 (60)
1948 21,811 (72)
1949 21,031 (76)
1950 22,680 (51)
1951 26,550 (19)
1952 26,500 (50)
1953 29,373 (30)
1954 27,600 (70)
1955 28,202 (78)
1956 29,625 (44)
1957 24,417 (53)
1958 24,010 (67)
1959 26,450
1960 28,881
Number of weekdays
out of service in brackets.
Includes works attention,
shed repairs/exams and
'not required'

Boilers
8406 new
21/9/39 8410 from 2978
12/6/45 6078 from 2946
1/7/50   6057 from 2954
26/3/55 6074

Repairs
30/1/36-25/2/36**LS**
4/6/37-18/6/37**LS**
10/9/37-21/10/37**LO**
5/7/39-21/9/39**HG**
29/7/41-16/8/41**HS**
16/9/43-16/10/43**LS**
18/3/44-20/4/44**LO**
12/4/45-12/6/45**HG**
6/2/48-12/3/48**HS**
8/9/49-2/11/49**NC**
22/5/50-1/7/50**HG**
21/3/52-19/4/52**LI**
1/3/54-15/4/54**LI**
10/2/55-23/3/55**HG**
24/6/57-3/8/57**LI**
20/8/59-7/10/59**LI**
3/62 **classification unknown**

Mileage at 12/36: 119,305
Mileage at 31/12/50: 443,539
Withdrawn w.e. 25/9/65
Cut up T.W. Ward, Beighton

2974 in an unusual view, hauling refurbished WD 2-8-0s 77014, 77378, 77421 and 77106 past Berkhamsted on 18 March 1947. All were destined for the GWR, it seems; approaching in the distance is Jubilee 5695 MINOTAUR. Photograph H.C. Casserley, courtesy R.M. Casserley.

42974, by now with a flush-sided tender, at rest and trundling round the yard at Crewe South shed on 24 June 1961. We're back now to the more conventional styling of the smokebox plate numbers. Annual mileages steadily declined over the years and by now of course the moguls were almost venerable, approaching thirty years in age. Moreover, longer distance fitted freights had been given over to Black Fives, 8Fs and then 9Fs, so both the Crabs and the Stanier moguls were constrained by a diet of the lower classes of freight. Photographs D. Forsyth, Paul Chancellor Collection.

42975

Built 25/1/34 as 13275
Renumbered 2975 21/11/35
Renumbered 42975 w.e. 12/6/48

Boilers

	8407	new
6/10/39	6076	from 2962
16/9/44	6074	from 2968
3/9/49	6058	from 2956
2/7/54	8403	
28/7/60	6055	

Tenders
4544 25/1/34
4520 29/9/37

Mileage
1934 40,158 (38)
1935 29,662 (104)
1936 36,788 (44)
1937 16,693 (175)
1938 26,485 (56)
1939 24,096 (90)
1940 28,184 (35)
1941 25,478 (74)
1942 26,912 (89)
1943 32,882 (24)
1944 23,630 (102)
1945 27,370 (59)
1946 27,594 (54)
1947 30,332 (68)
1948 30,365 (83)
1949 24,697 (107)
1950 29,726 (48)
1951 29,821 (67)
1952 28,656 (48)
1953 30,673 (59)
1954 23,642 (100)
1955 29,278 (59)
1956 29,370 (54)
1957 25,506 (71)
1958 26,698 (101)
1959 30,508
1960 19,271
Number of weekdays
out of service in brackets.
Includes works attention,
shed repairs/exams and
'not required'

Repairs
17/10/35-21/11/35**LS**
31/3/37-8/6/37**HS**
28/9/37-12/11/37**HO**
6/10/39-23/11/39**HG**
17/9/41-4/10/41**HS**
12/10/42-28/11/42**LS**
20/3/44-25/3/44**LO**
11/8/44-16/9/44**HG**
17/12/46-25/1/47**LS**
12/5/48-12/6/48**HS**
27/6/49-3/9/49**HG**
11/10/51-6/11/51**HI**
29/12/52-14/1/53**LC**
15/5/54-2/7/54**HG**
6/10/54-29/10/54**LC(EO)**
16/3/56-18/4/56**HI**
24/1/58-1/3/58**LI**
17/11/58-4/12/58**LC(TO)**
2/5/60-28/7/60**HG**
17/2/61-28/3/61**LC(EO)**
6/64-9/64 **Swindon**

Sheds
Crewe South
Holyhead*
Newton Heath by 5/34
Birkenhead 1/6/35
Chester 11/7/36
Birkenhead 3/7/37
Edge Hill 26/11/38
Willesden 3/5/41
Mold Junction 8/11/41
Willesden 10/5/58
Aston 20/6/59
Stockport Edgeley 17/9/60
Crewe South 22/10/60
Rugby 31/12/60
Nuneaton 21/1/61
Bescot 18/5/63
Gorton 2/1/65
Heaton Mersey 12/6/65
date omitted; probably erroneous

Mileage at 12/36: 106,608
Mileage at 31/12/50: 481,052
Withdrawn w.e. 26/3/66
Cut up J. Cashmore, Great Bridge

42975 at Mold Junction, something of a stronghold for the class over the years, on 29 July 1951. The place was obscure but its importance lay in its yards and role as freight shed for the Chester area, with its North Wales links. It was close to Chester (and a lot further from Mold) and was effectively the freight pivot for all LNW lines to the west and Ireland, leaving Chester shed itself to concentrate more on passenger work. If it had been called 'Chester West' (perhaps not – that was GW) there might have been a generally clearer idea of its importance. There was a lot of heavy plodding and relatively short distance work, with intense summer holiday peaks, so a stud of Stanier moguls was a handy thing to have. A fireman at Mold Junction told Eric Youldon in 1963 that it was the 'healthiest shed in the Division' on account of the stiff breeze that blew constantly across it! Photograph B.K.B. Green, Initial Photographics.

Handy as in this case, in which 42975 is at Rhyl station with – once again – an August Bank Holiday special, this time a Newcastle-Llandudno working, on 31 July 1954. Photograph B.K.B. Green, Initial Photographics.

42975 at Bolton shed, 5 August 1960. Oddly (as mentioned) for a class maintained entirely at Horwich, they were allocated almost anywhere *but* the sheds of the former Central Division, which corresponded more or less to the old L&Y; she is here because Bolton tended to serve as the running-in base for engines off Horwich. Other works had sheds adjacent – Crewe, Doncaster and so on – where an eye could be kept on an overhauled loco while it 'bedded in' its moving parts on gentle work for a few days. Photograph Norman Preedy.

42975 at Stockport Edgeley station, 30 September 1960, on another special and looking every bit 'up for the part'. Coal is piled on its original riveted tender – and good quality passenger stuff at that for the job in prospect. As can be seen, the Stanier hooter arrived with this one. Photograph D. Forsyth, Paul Chancellor Collection.

42976

Built 24/1/34 as 13276
Renumbered 2976 1/8/34
Renumbered 42976 w.e. 5/3/49

Tenders
4545 24/1/34

Repairs
21/6/34-1/8/34**LO**
22/4/36-22/5/36**LS**
9/7/37-2/8/37**LS**
5/12/38-21/1/39**HG**
13/9/40-5/10/40**LS**
29/12/41-31/1/42**HS**
16/11/43-31/12/43**HG**
14/11/45-8/12/45**LS**
30/10/46-18/1/47**LO**
21/11/47-10/1/48**HG**
19/2/49-5/3/49**LC**
11/8/49-3/9/49**LI**
16/1/50-4/2/50**LO**
11/6/51-10/7/51**HG**
1/12/52-9/1/53**HI**
3/10/53-23/10/53**LC**
28/2/55-2/4/55**LI**
24/5/56-4/7/56**HG**
5/9/56-22/9/56**LC(EO)**
27/10/58-27/11/58**LI**
18/4/61-30/5/61**HI**
14/6/61-22/6/61**NC(EO)**
7/63 **classification unknown**

Mileage
1934 34,819 (64)
1935 34,427 (52)
1936 31,703 (50)
1937 30,211 (47)
1938 24,840 (95)
1939 29,090 (56)
1940 25,762 (68)
1941 37,900 (43)
1942 43,656 (66)
1943 32,433 (62)
1944 36,382 (47)
1945 28,300 (80)
1946 31,343 (77)
1947 23,440 (115)
1948 33,657 (46)
1949 25,965 (82)
1950 26,257 (59)
1951 26,815 (71)
1952 28,460 (61)
1953 32,695 (51)
1954 31,399 (37)
1955 29,308 (75)
1956 26,479 (83)
1957 29,843 (37)
1958 23,674 (75)
1959 33,979
1960 24,416
Number of weekdays
out of service in brackets.
Includes works attention,
shed repairs/exams and
'not required'

Boilers
        8408 new
26/1/39   6058 from 2952
31/12/43 6075 from 2951
10/1/48 8406 from 2971
10/7/51 8400 from 2945
4/7/56   8411

Sheds
Crewe South
Newton Heath by 4/34
Holyhead 25/5/35
Birkenhead 1/6/35
Edge Hill 3/7/37
Birkenhead 25/9/37
Chester 12/10/40
Birkenhead 22/2/41
Chester 5/4/41
Mold Junction 30/1/43
Chester 28/8/43
Llandudno Junction 14/7/45
Speke Junction 13/9/47
Mold Junction 25/10/47
Bescot 3/8/57
Mold Junction 17/8/57
Preston 23/4/60
Nuneaton 9/9/61

Mileage at 12/36: 100,949
Mileage at 31/12/50: 530,185
Withdrawn w.e. 20/7/63
Cut up Horwich

One of the classic haunts of the class, the North Wales coast line. This is the sea wall at Penmaenmawr and Mold Junction's 42976 has freight bound for Holyhead, on 1 September 1953. Photograph R.E. Vincent, The Transport Treasury.

On the new turntable at Crewe North, 25 June 1960. When the grand old shed got its mechanical plants in the 1950s there were to have been two modern roundhouses as well but the project was cut back to leave only this lightly-built (a bit ropey to be honest) semi-roundhouse. Photograph D. Forsyth, Paul Chancellor Collection.

42977

Built 23/1/34 as 13277
Renumbered 2977 12/3/36
Renumbered 42977 w.e. 16/10/48

Boilers

	8409 new
27/12/37	6081 from 2965
25/4/42	6053 from 2984
29/11/46	8411 from 2963
2/5/51	9246 from 2973
7/6/56	6083

Tenders
4546 23/1/34

Mileage
1934 34,792 (72)
1935 34,458 (51)
1936 35,179 (77)
1937 38,321 (87)
1938 28,035 (92)
1939 25,349 (91)
1940 20,521 (59)
1941 24,433 (58)
1942 23,149 (67)
1943 24,063 (41)
1944 18,769 (67)
1945 21,423 (86)
1946 15,385 (116)
1947 23,841 (51)
1948 20,576 (89)
1949 22,758 (46)
1950 18,713 (65)
1951 19,821 (59)
1952 20,760 (53)
1953 20,778 (67)
1954 22,288 (49)
1955 19,616 (71)
1956 20,497 (92)
1957 18,670 (57)
1958 21,898 (75)
1959 24,738
1960 23,557
Number of weekdays
out of service in brackets.
Includes works attention,
shed repairs/exams and
'not required'

Sheds
Crewe South
Newton Heath by 5/34
Holyhead 25/5/35
Birkenhead 1/6/35
Carlisle Upperby 1/4/36
Nuneaton 25/9/37
Crewe South 5/7/47
Speke Junction 27/11/48
Birkenhead 20/10/51
Rugby 3/12/60
Nuneaton 21/1/61
Crewe South 4/3/61
Bushbury 18/8/62
Stoke 15/12/62
Springs Branch 14/12/63
Gorton 15/5/65
Heaton Mersey 12/6/65

Repairs
8/2/36-12/3/36**LS**
18/3/36-1/4/36**LO**
19/11/36-25/11/36**LO**
25/10/37-31/12/37**HG**
9/7/40-23/7/40**LS**
11/3/42-25/4/42**HG**
2/8/44-26/8/44**LS**
15/7/45-31/8/45**LO**
28/8/46-29/11/46**HS**
27/8/48-16/10/48**HS**
7/3/50-31/3/50**LC**
22/3/51-2/5/51**HG**
4/2/54-26/2/54**LI**
23/4/56-7/6/56**HG**
25/2/58-29/3/58**HI**
9/6/60-2/8/60**HI**
31/1/61-24/2/61**LC**
18/9/61-3/10/61**NC(EO)**
6/63 classification unknown

Mileage at 12/36: 104,429
Mileage at 31/12/50: 429,765
Withdrawn w.e. 18/6/66
Cut up Birds, Long Marston

The Sketchley dye workers get a deserved day out behind 2977 in 1938. The destination is not known but this is Elstree on the Midland (that's the studios in the background) and the train is heading south.

If there was a spiritual home for the Stanier moguls it was probably Crewe South; 42977 is on shed there on 22 August 1959. She looks a bit deadbeat and is a long time away from her last General. This was when defects would show at their worst, late in an engine's life and late in a repair cycle. Coupled wheel springs, for instance, would become weak and the boxes might hit the top of the horn guides on rough track but springs fracturing or going 'soft', with subsequent rough riding, happened with all engines. The sheds combated it by replacing or 'charging' some springs between shoppings. Photograph D. Forsyth, Paul Chancellor Collection.

Stockport Edgeley station, 16 May 1961 and 42977 is on some motley stock duty. Still with riveted tender and probably first emblem too. In latter years the exhaust steam injector (on the right-hand side; live steam at this side) seems generally to have given more trouble than it should, a situation presumably due to declining maintenance; it was the sort of annoying deficiency that could afflict any class in the regime of neglect that evolved in the 1960s. Photograph D. Forsyth, Paul Chancellor Collection.

Classic portrait at Crewe South shed, 23 June 1962. Blanking plates for the mudhole doors (no longer fitted) visible on firebox shoulders. Photograph C. Smith, Paul Chancellor Collection.

42978

Built 25/1/34 as 13278
Renumbered 2978 22/7/35
Renumbered 42978 w.e.27/11/48

Boilers

	8410 new
3/7/39	8408 from 2976
3/12/43	8412 from 2952
20/3/52	9247
6/4/57	8406

Tenders
4547 25/1/34
4521 27/11/48
3694 4/6/56

Sheds
Crewe South
Huddersfield 19/5/34
Rose Grove 3/11/34
Holyhead 25/5/35
Birkenhead 1/6/35
Edge Hill 26/11/38
Willesden 3/5/41
Edge Hill 10/5/41
Chester 17/1/42
Mold Junction 2/5/42
Edge Hill 14/11/42
Speke Junction 27/10/45
Longsight 19/11/49
Aston 21/7/51
Crewe South 3/11/51
Birkenhead 5/7/52
Rugby 3/12/60
Nuneaton 21/1/61
Mold Junction 22/6/63
Birkenhead 5/10/63
Nuneaton 26/10/63
Gorton 2/1/65
Heaton Mersey 12/6/65

Mileage
1934 39,389 (40)
1935 29,488 (68)
1936 34,179 (60)
1937 29,381 (54)
1938 28,229 (65)
1939 30,283 (80)
1940 26,235 (59)
1941 26,295 (58)
1942 35,005 (29)
1943 25,973 (59)
1944 30,655 (26)
1945 23,552 (68)
1946 20,821 (40)
1947 19,934 (91)
1948 8,075 (189)
1949 23,675 (46)
1950 21,173 (80)
1951 24,262 (51)
1952 25,569 (60)
1953 20,493 (65)
1954 20,038 (64)
1955 23,182 (64)
1956 19,898 (59)
1957 22,324 (57)
1958 22,508 (34)
1959 23,626
1960 22,442
Number of weekdays
out of service in brackets.
Includes works attention,
shed repairs/exams and
'not required'

Repairs
4/6/35-22/7/35**LS**
27/5/37-28/5/37**LO**
14/2/38-19/3/38**HS**
17/5/39-3/7/39**HG**
18/6/40-20/7/40**LS**
31/10/41-28/11/41**HS**
4/11/43-3/12/43**HG**
31/8/45-6/10/45**LS**
29/5/48-27/11/48**HG**
27/11/50-6/1/51**LI**
11/2/52-20/3/52**HG**
4/9/54-7/10/54**HI**
26/2/57-6/4/57**HG**
20/8/59-8/10/59**LI**
31/3/60-26/5/60**LC(EO)**
13/6/61-23/6/61**NC(EO)**
5/64 **Swindon**

Mileage at 12/36: 102,956
Mileage at 31/12/50: 452,242
Withdrawn w.e. 30/4/66
Cut up Birds, Long Marston

42978 in an unlikely spot, Brimscombe. It is just pulling out of the loop on to the main line, banker attached, for the long climb up to Sapperton. Photograph Norman Preedy.

42979 at Crewe South shed, 22 August 1959, in company with one of the new diesel shunters. These too, soon acquired the grey-grime livery of classes such as the Stanier moguls. Firebox 'shoulder patches' again. Photograph D. Forsyth, Paul Chancellor Collection.

42979

Built 2/2/34 as 13279
Renumbered 2979 25/7/35
Renumbered 42979 w.e. 4/12/48

Tenders
4548 2/2/34

Sheds
Crewe South
Huddersfield 19/5/34
Rose Grove 3/11/34
Crewe South 25/5/35
Warrington 9/11/35
Springs Branch 13/11/37
Birkenhead 5/3/38
Chester 12/10/40
Mold Junction 8/11/41
Speke Junction 4/12/48
Longsight 19/11/49
Aston 13/6/53
Crewe South 26/9/53
Aston 31/10/53
Birkenhead 18/5/57 (loan)
Aston 1/6/57
Stockport Edgeley 17/9/60
Crewe South 22/10/60
Aston 26/11/60
Bescot 23/6/62

Mileage
1934 39,106 (24)
1935 28,964 (91)
1936 29,638 (69)
1937 28,332 (76)
1938 24,909 (104)
1939 29,588 (53)
1940 25,673 (56)
1941 32,247 (44)
1942 26,042 (83)
1943 33,870 (29)
1944 26,500 (60)
1945 21,861 (100)
1946 32,160 (42)
1947 22,891 (124)
1948 30,661(78)
1949 26,663 (30)
1950 23,100 (53)
1951 26,054 (67)
1952 23,971 (80)
1953 30,226 (29)
1954 27,907 (44)
1955 25,949 (54)
1956 25,097 (45)
1957 22,547 (99)
1958 25,409 (34)
1959 21,735
1960 28,679
*Number of weekdays
out of service in brackets.
Includes works attention,
shed repairs/exams and
'not required'*

Boilers
	8411 new
5/5/38	6060 from 2954
11/4/42	9248 from 2947
31/5/47	6053 from 2977
12/11/52	8412
3/7/57	6079

Repairs
30/5/35-25/7/35**LS**
3/3/36-21/4/36**LO**
30/6/37-27/7/37**LS**
2/3/38-17/5/38**HG**
15/7/40-3/8/40**HS**
19/2/42-11/4/42**HG**
15/2/44-11/3/44**LS**
23/10/45-1/12/45**LS**
21/2/47-31/5/47**HG**
29/10/48-4/12/48**HS**
20/9/50-12/10/50**HI**
15/9/52-12/11/52**HG**
5/10/54-4/11/54**HI**
5/12/55-14/1/56**LC**
4/6/57-3/7/57**HG**
26/8/57-20/9/57**LC(EO)**
15/10/59-20/11/59**LI**
4/62 **classification unknown**

Mileage at 12/36: 97,708
Mileage at 31/12/50: 487,205
Withdrawn w.e. 5/12/64
Cut up T.W. Ward, Beighton

Another excellent portrait from the Edgeley footpath, 30 August 1961; AWS now, along with electrification flashes. There was also, it seems, a 'warning notice' on 'low fronted tenders' such as these; fire irons were customarily stowed on top of the coal in the absence of a 'tunnel' at the side (as in the case of the Stanier 4,000 gallon tenders) and it was easy to get too near the 25kV wires. The cost was £4, which presumably covered front and aft flashes too. Photograph D. Forsyth, Paul Chancellor Collection.

At home at Bescot shed, with the code 21B painted on, 28 July 1962. Photograph D. Forsyth, Paul Chancellor Collection.

42980

Built 7/2/34 as 13280
Renumbered 2980 29/7/35
Renumbered 42980 w.e.8/10/49

Tenders
4549 7/2/34

Repairs
24/5/34-22/6/34**LO**
14/5/35-29/7/35**HS**
4/1/37-18/1/37**LS**
30/8/37-11/9/37**LO**
2/4/38-25/5/38**HG**
8/7/40-20/7/40**HS**
5/8/42-18/9/42**HG**
11/9/44-14/10/44**LS**
14/3/47-21/6/47**HG**
15/9/49-7/10/49**LI**
3/12/49-23/12/49**LC**
28/1/50-11/2/50**LC**
13/9/51-11/10/51**HG**
20/10/51-23/10/51**Rect**
11/1/54-10/2/54**LI**
24/9/56-9/11/56**HG**
14/3/58-11/4/58**LI**
26/11/59-7/12/59**NC(EO)**
29/3/60-20/5/60**LI**
6/63 **classification unknown**
10/63 **classification unknown**

Mileage
1934 34,545 (54)
1935 24,087 (133)
1936 40,013 (38)
1937 30,910 (67)
1938 19,011 (90)
1939 27,073 (31)
1940 28,025 (50)
1941 26,414 (43)
1942 25,504 (91)
1943 30,241 (41)
1944 22,216 (80)
1945 29,949 (27)
1946 26,321 (50)
1947 18,952 (138)
1948 24,237 (68)
1949 20,030 (94)
1950 31,820 (53)
1951 28,038 (50)
1952 31,058 (57)
1953 26,831 (46)
1954 29,818 (54)
1955 18,798 (129)
1956 18,953 (124)
1957 30,627 (41)
1958 29,384 (57)
1959 29,063
1960 26,249
Number of weekdays
out of service in brackets.
Includes works attention,
shed repairs/exams and
'not required'

Boilers
　　　　8412 new
16/5/38　8402 from 2970
18/9/42　6056 from 2981
21/6/47　6059 from 2953
11/10/51　8410
9/11/56　6077

Sheds
Newton Heath
Crewe South 12/5/34
Edge Hill 19/1/35
Bescot 7/3/36
Monument Lane 25/4/36
Aston 20/3/37
Monument Lane 12/6/37
Bescot 25/9/37
Bangor 17/2/40
Aston (loan) 9/3/40
Bangor 20/7/40
Crewe South 11/1/41
Birkenhead 18/5/57
Crewe South 3/8/57
Stoke 24/11/62
Bescot 9/3/63
Stoke 22/6/63
Gorton 5/12/64
Heaton Mersey 12/6/65

Mileage at 12/36: 98,645
Mileage at 31/12/50: 459,248
Withdrawn w.e. 8/1/66
Cut up T.W. Ward, Killamarsh

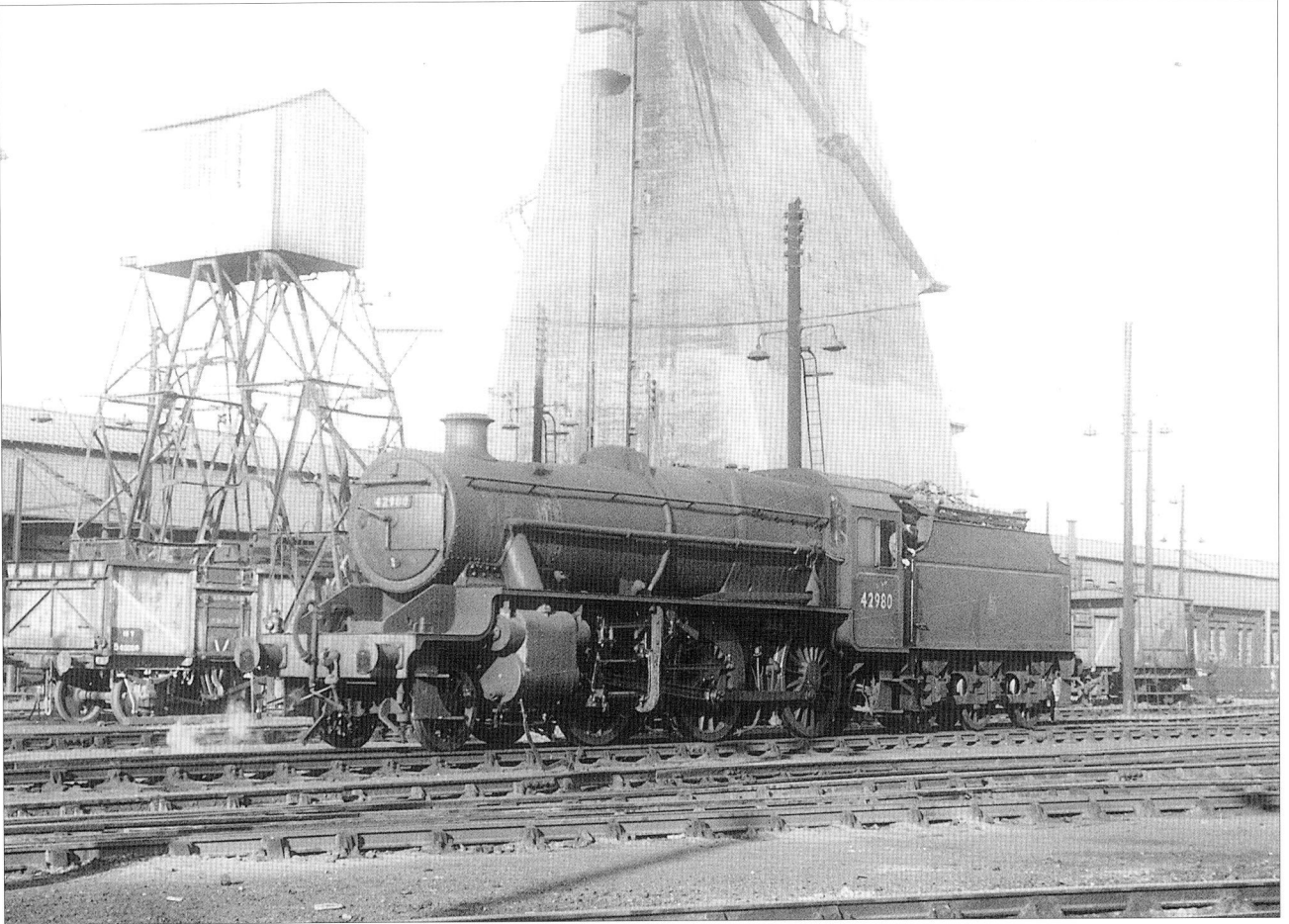

42980 up in town and in front of the giant coaling plant at Willesden, 24 July 1958. Photograph H.C. Casserley, courtesy R.M. Casserley.

42980 rolls back through Stockport Edgeley station on 29 July 1959. Photograph D. Forsyth, Paul Chancellor Collection.

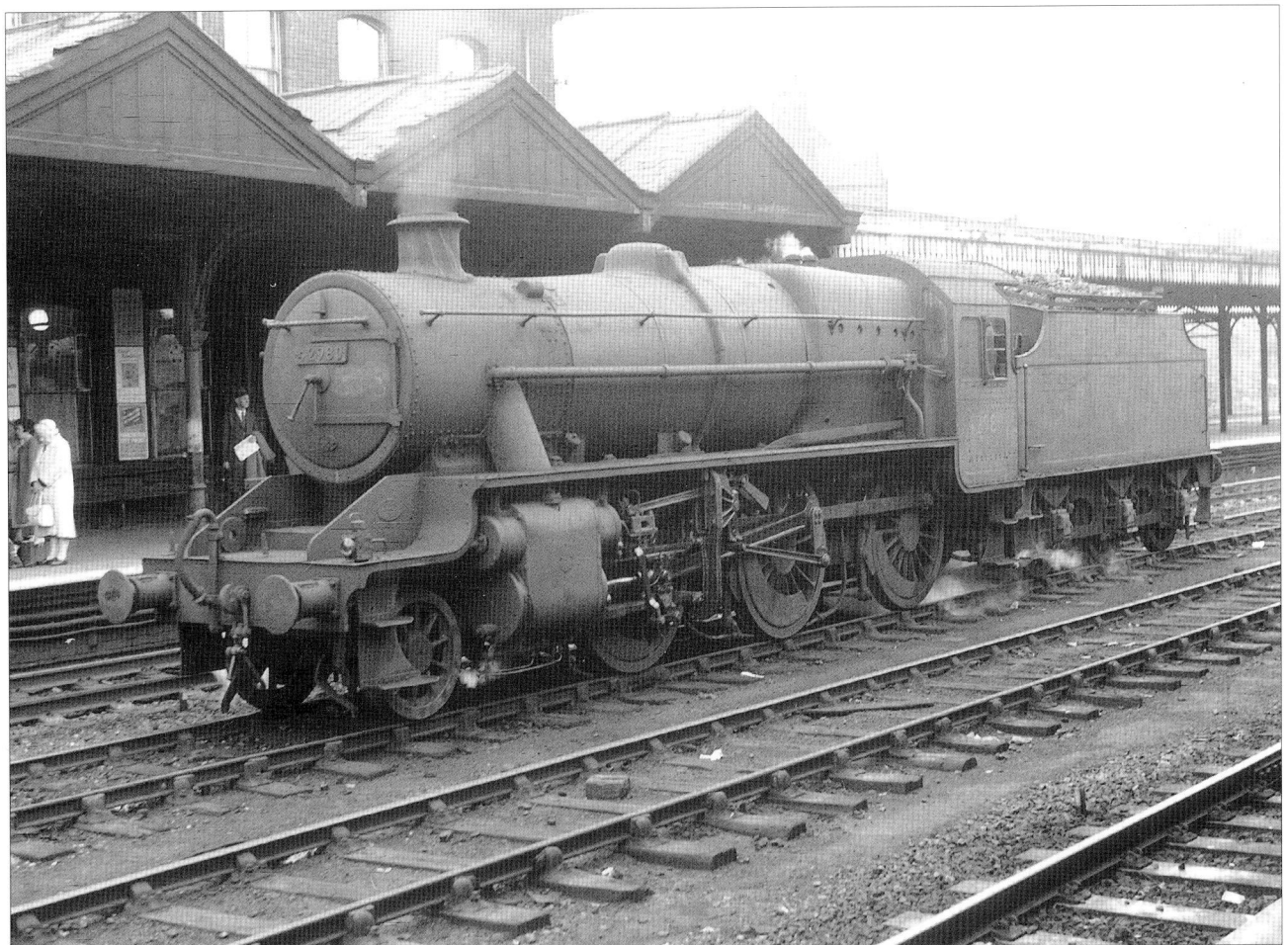

42981

Built 12/2/34 as 13281
Renumbered 2981 27/5/35
Renumbered 42981 w.e. 6/8/49

Tenders
4550 12/2/34
4201 8/7/49
4538 26/5/55

Boilers

	8413 new
23/6/38	6056 from 2950
5/9/42	6073 from 2982
24/1/48	8403 from 2968
10/12/53	6054
24/2/61	6082

Repairs
16/3/35-27/5/35**HS**
5/6/35-23/7/35**LO**
7/4/37-12/4/37**LO**
9/6/37-18/6/37**LO**
29/7/37-19/8/37**LS**
13/5/38-28/6/38**HG**
8/6/40-25/6/40**LS**
3/7/42-5/9/42**HG**
3/6/43-6/7/43**TRO**
31/8/44-23/9/44**LO**
27/6/45-11/8/45**LS**
15/1/46-9/2/46**LO**
4/12/47-24/1/48**HG**
31/1/48-5/2/48**Rect**
28/6/49-6/8/49**LI**
17/11/49-9/12/49**LC**
20/8/51-27/9/51**LI**
3/5/52-29/5/52**HC**
15/10/53-10/12/53**HG**
25/1/56-3/3/56**LI**
26/7/56-18/8/56**HC(EO)**
28/7/58-12/9/58**LI**
8/5/59-3/6/59**LC(TO)**
12/1/60-2/2/60**LC**
19/12/60-24/2/61**HG**
1/3/61-6/3/61**NC(EO)**
23/10/61-2/11/61**NC(EO)**
2/62 **classification unknown**
6/63 **classification unknown**

Mileage
1934 32,856 (76)
1935 26,482 (134)
1936 35,224 (63)
1937 26,751 (66)
1938 24,619 (80)
1939 25,964 (97)
1940 27,673 (56)
1941 21,568 (82)
1942 18,297 (87)
1943 25,731 (54)
1944 16,698 (88)
1945 18,939 (76)
1946 20,043 (56)
1947 20,790 (70)
1948 20,005 (108)
1949 16,884 (111)
1950 22,352 (25)
1951 17,206 (94)
1952 21,090 (58)
1953 20,043 (95)
1954 27,313 (38)
1955 21,173 (73)
1956 21,345 (90)
1957 24,041 (42)
1958 19,738 (92)
1959 30,418
1960 21,574
Number of weekdays
out of service in brackets.
Includes works attention,
shed repairs/exams and
'not required'

Sheds
Newton Heath
Crewe South 12/5/34
Aston 6/6/36
Willesden 14/11/36
Bushbury 27/3/37
Aston 3/7/37
Bescot 25/9/37
Springs Branch 2/7/38
Edge Hill 5/11/38
Nuneaton 29/3/41
Birkenhead 5/3/49
Mold Junction 22/11/58
Birkenhead 18/6/60
Nuneaton 16/6/62
Crewe South 22/6/63
Rugby 9/11/63
Gorton 2/1/65
Heaton Mersey 12/6/65

Mileage at 12/36: 94,562
Mileage at 31/12/50: 400,876
Withdrawn w.e. 21/5/66
Cut up G. Cohen, Rotherham

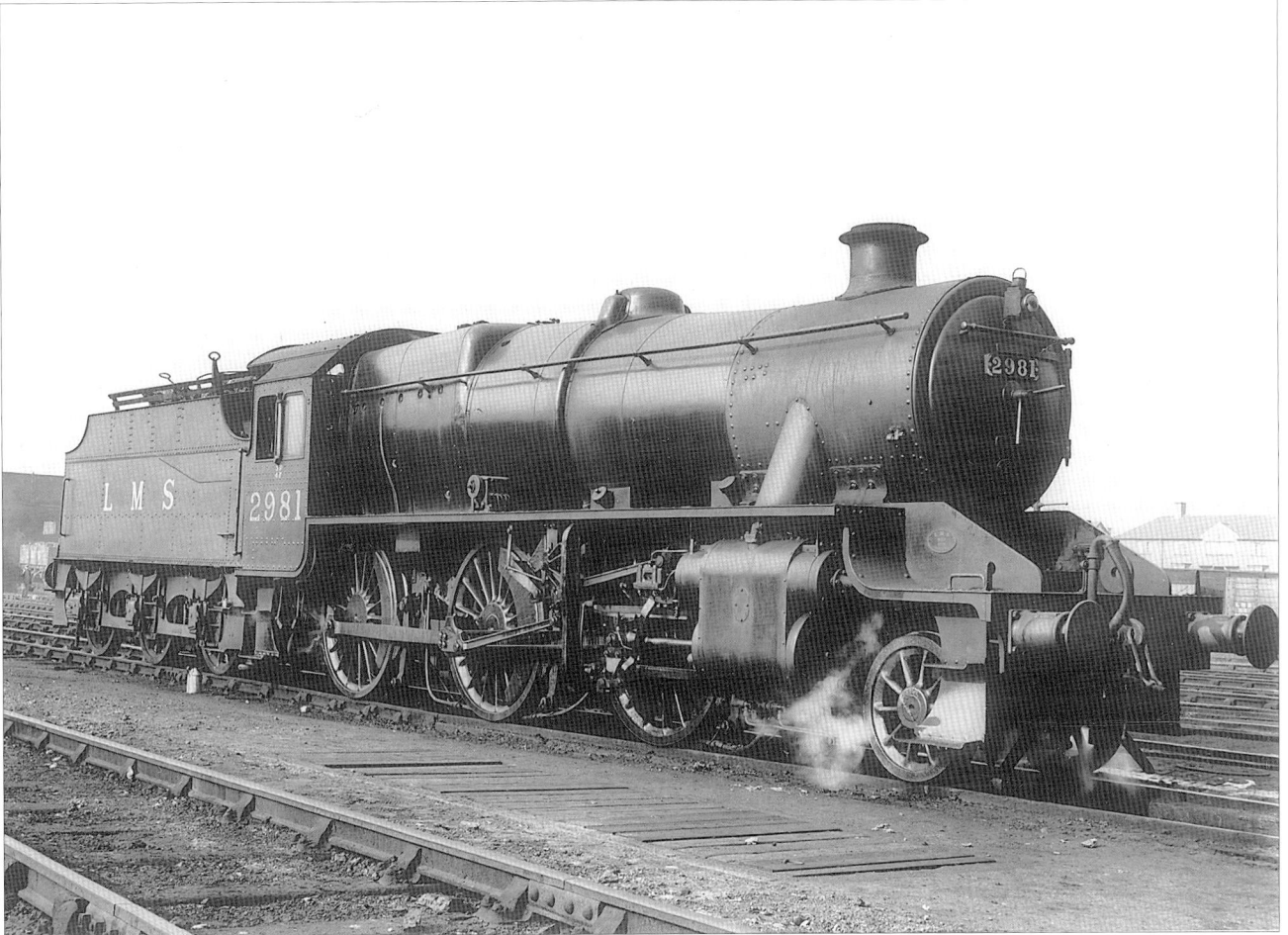

As good as it gets for a mogul! This is the shed yard at Bushbury, almost certainly just after 2981's Heavy General in 1938; Bescot (3A) shed plate. Photograph Kidderminster Railway Museum, L.W. Perkins/A. Wycherley Collection.

Below. A bright, clean 42980 at Bolton shed, 29 June 1963. Its condition and location indicate a visit to Horwich, one that came unfortunately too late to be entered in the Engine History Card. With work transferred to Swindon from the end of the year this would have been one of the last Horwich repairs. In the course of it she has managed to re-acquire a riveted tender, now with second emblem. On a visit to Horwich on 7 August 1963 Eric Youldon found 42952, 42955 and 42977 all going through; 42976, withdrawn the previous month, was also present. Photograph D. Forsyth, Paul Chancellor Collection.

More familiar guise of grime, 42981 at Chester shed, 10 July 1962. Photograph R.Reed.

42982

Built 8/2/34 as 13282
Renumbered 2982 16/4/35
Renumbered 42982 w.e. 23/10/48

Tenders
4551 8/2/34
3665 14/11/55

Repairs
4/3/35-16/4/35**HS**
28/10/35-26/11/35**HO**
9/7/36-22/7/36**LO**
13/7/37-11/9/37**HG**
8/1/40-23/2/40**HS**
13/5/41-2/6/41**LO**
8/12/41-31/1/42**HG**
20/3/44-22/4/44**LS**
14/5/45-30/6/45**HO**
17/12/46-25/1/47**HS**
8/6/48-23/10/48**HG**
14/2/50-23/5/50**HI**
20/8/52-27/9/52**LI**
26/10/54-29/11/54**HG**
7/11/55-30/11/55**LC**
18/2/57-23/3/57**HI**
9/2/59-15/4/59**LI**
12/61 **classification unknown**
5/62 **classification unknown**

Mileage
1934 33,842 (66)
1935 32,537 (105)
1936 36,274 (38)
1937 23,312 (93)
1938 36,123 (45)
1939 28,515 (39)
1940 20,762 (74)
1941 22,079 (76)
1942 25,471 (68)
1943 26,861 (41)
1944 22,566 (61)
1945 18,548 (115)
1946 28,742 (51)
1947 26,587 (73)
1948 13,468 (165)
1949 22,003 (26)
1950 20,328 (73)
1951 23,977 (53)
1952 25,571 (68)
1953 29,897 (55)
1954 26,376 (62)
1955 29,200 (69)
1956 31,236 (41)
1957 28,240 (53)
1958 26,475 (53)
1959 27,298
1960 20,469
Number of weekdays
out of service in brackets.
Includes works attention,
shed repairs/exams and
'not required'

Boilers
	8414 new
7/9/37	6073 from 2957
31/1/42	8400 from 2949
30/6/45	6072 from 2959
23/10/48	6071 from 2951
20/11/54	6051

Sheds
Newton Heath
Crewe South 12/5/34
Willesden 19/1/35
Edge Hill 20/4/35
Bescot 7/3/36
Monument Lane 25/4/36
Walsall 11/7/36
Birkenhead 2/1/37
Edge Hill 3/7/37
Warrington 3/7/37
Crewe South 5/7/41
Speke Junction 4/12/48
Mold Junction 2/2/52
Aston 18/6/60
Mold Junction 4/2/61
Chester 16/6/61
Nuneaton 16/6/62
Gorton 2/1/65
Heaton Mersey 12/6/65

Mileage at 12/36: 102,653
Mileage at 31/12/50: 438,018
Withdrawn w.e. 13/11/65
Cut up J. Cashmore, Great Bridge

42982 with, unusually, no trace of a shed plate, at Willesden about 1962. Electrification flash on tender front. Only part of the fine BR lined black livery shows through and it is a sadness that neglect rarely allowed locos such as these to show of their best. There was a very attractive livery under all that. Photograph J.G. Walmsley, The Transport Treasury.

42983

Built 9/3/34 as 13283
Renumbered 2983 1/7/35
Renumbered 42983 w.e. 25/9/48

Tenders
4552 9/3/34

Repairs
5/5/35-1/7/35**HO**
5/12/35-24/1/36**LS**
26/6/36-27/6/36**LO**
5/10/37-12/11/37**HG**
11/1/40-10/2/40**HS**
7/8/41-23/8/41**LS**
25/8/42-5/9/42**TRO**
4/7/43-11/9/43**HG**
29/5/45-30/6/45**LS**
25/11/46-11/1/47**HS**
16/6/48-25/9/48**HG**
6/6/50-30/6/50**LI**
4/4/52-6/5/52**HI**
26/5/53-18/8/53**HG**
9/8/54-28/8/54**LC(EO)**
25/1/56-1/3/56**LI**
22/2/57-16/3/57**LC(EO)**
2/10/58-28/11/58**HG**
11/11/59-30/11/59**NC(EO)**
11/12/59-19/1/60**LC(EO)**
12/61 **classification unknown**
1/64-3/64 **classification unknown**

Mileage
1934 36,971 (37)
1935 32,950 (120)
1936 35,183 (59)
1937 20,755 (98
1938 36,960 (45)
1939 30,388 (62)
1940 24,966 (73)
1941 22,078 (66)
1942 24,164 (33)
1943 19,682 (85)
1944 26,140 (41)
1945 24,500 (67)
1946 19,563 (72)
1947 24,933 (69)
1948 18,866 (128)
1949 31,092 (47)
1950 30,080 (54)
1951 28,733 (49)
1952 29,154 (55)
1953 22,349 (95)
1954 29,956 (54)
1955 27,892 (45)
1956 29,010 (73)
1957 23,002 (79)
1958 23,732 (97)
1959 30,267
1960 30,820
Number of weekdays
out of service in brackets.
Includes works attention,
shed repairs/exams and
'not required'

Boilers
8415 new
2/11/37 6083 from 2967
11/9/43 6051 from 2958
25/9/48 8402 from 2965
18/8/53 6056
28/11/58 8409

Sheds
Newton Heath
Crewe South 12/5/34
Aston 6/6/36
Willesden 14/11/36
Bescot 9/1/37
Aston 3/7/37
Abergavenny 24/9/38
Shrewsbury 8/10/38
Crewe South 26/11/38
Longsight 4/10/41
Crewe South 29/8/42
Bushbury 18/7/64
Oxley 17/4/65
Heaton Mersey 12/65

Mileage at 12/36: 105,104
Mileage at 31/12/50: 459,271
Withdrawn w.e. 15/1/66
Cut up T.W. Ward, Killamarsh

Climbing near Shap Wells, 42983 looks in good condition – for an engine in the lower ranks of freight working at least, with front end repaint. It was at Crewe South throughout virtually its entire BR existence; the train is probably the 7.40am 'H' Crewe Basford Hall-Carlisle London Road, booked for a Crewe South Black Five.

42983 rushes along the Up Slow on the south end of the LNW. DC electric lines are to the left.

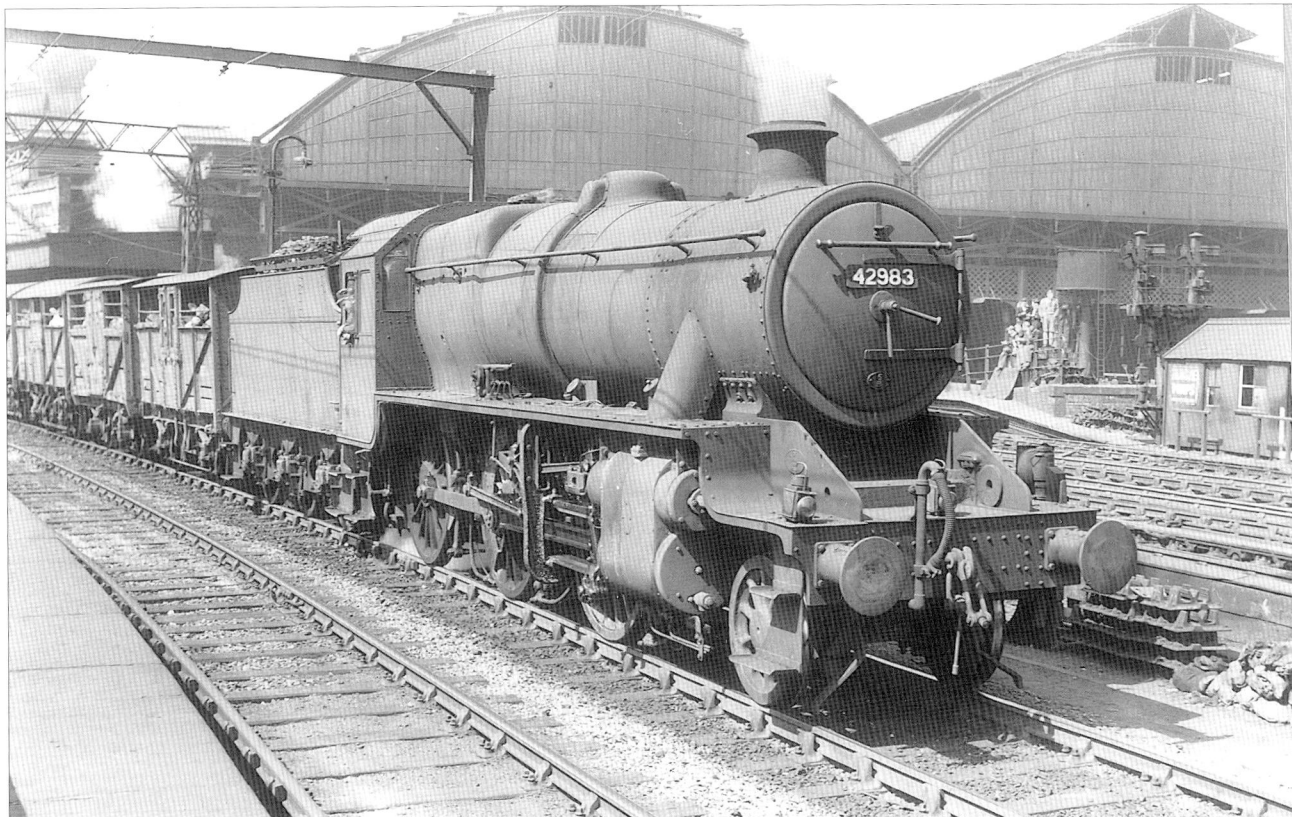

42983 at Manchester London Road with a cattle train off the Chester line, 24 April 1951. The Stanier moguls were in theory more than a match for the Black Fives though in practice this never worked out so. Steaming could never be quite so assured and they were never habitually put on main line passenger work. The critical fact was that they could never match the Black Fives across the whole *range* of duties and in that sense they were not so useful, whatever the power classification might say. At all those unsung sheds where they performed, equally unsung, day after day, that was where they proved their worth. Photograph B.K.B. Green, Initial Photographics.

42983 at Swindon (it is believed) in 1964; some parts are painted, others not. She was one of the first to go to Swindon under the arrangements of '12.63' as the scrawl on the Engine History Cards puts it. Along with 42954 she was there in January 1964 and was undergoing attention by March. From various reports there only seem to have been eight Stanier moguls dealt with at Swindon; 42945, 42953, 42958, 42961, 42975 and 42978 were the others. There were quite a few more 43000 and 76000 moguls from the LMR but by early the following year, 1965, there was no steam at all at Swindon. Oddly, 42978 turned up on Swindon shed in September 1964 but it is not known whether this was a chance visit or it had been sent for works attention. As with the last ten, 42983 has the Stanier 'hooter' and, like the last five, it has the single lubricator on the running plate.

42984

Built 7/3/34 as 13284
Renumbered 2984 3/5/35
Renumbered 42984 w.e. 16/10/48

Boilers

	8416 new
17/6/37	6053 from 2947
28/2/42	6054 from 2943
27/9/47	8413 from 2969
2/5/52	8416
17/8/56	9246

Tenders
4553 7/3/34
4125 22/12/53
3595 10/8/54
4125 28/9/54

Repairs
5/3/35-3/5/35**HS**
10/4/37-22/6/37**HG**
29/7/39-8/9/39**LS**
12/3/41-15/4/41**TRO**
6/2/42-28/2/42**HG**
28/1/44-4/3/44**LS**
18/12/45-2/2/46**LS**
22/4/47-27/9/47**HG**
8/10/47-10/10/47**Rect**
5/3/48-15/3/48**NC**
17/9/48-15/10/48**HO**
25/5/49-9/6/49**LC**
27/1/50-25/2/50**LI**
3/3/51-21/3/51**LC**
26/3/52-2/5/52**HG**
22/12/53-21/1/54**LI**
23/6/56-17/8/56**HG**
21/8/56-29/8/56**NC(Rect)**
14/9/57-28/9/57**LC**
10/11/58-23/12/58**HI**
28/19/59-6/11/59**NC(EO)**
7/12/59-21/1/60**LC(EO)**
27/1/61-24/3/61**LI**
25/3/61-4/4/61**NC(Rect)EO**

Mileage
1934 36,147 (45)
1935 35,940 (86)
1936 34,936 (56)
1937 23,650 (101)
1938 25,687 (54)
1939 25,894 (77)
1940 35,410 (26)
1941 19,332 (105)
1942 29,271 (38)
1943 28,551 (64)
1944 29,433 (74)
1945 28,433 (74)
1946 31,704 (72)
1947 18,356 (166)
1948 24,070 (62)
1949 24,704 (61)
1950 30,233 (69)
1951 28,164 (62)
1952 25,700 (84)
1953 26,753 (72)
1954 26,276 (61)
1955 26,669 (58)
1956 22,876 (81)
1957 30,878 (38)
1958 27,241 (73)
1959 31,581
1960 26,746
Number of weekdays out of service in brackets. Includes works attention, shed repairs/exams and 'not required'

Sheds
Newton Heath
Crewe South 12/5/34
Willesden 19/1/35
Edge Hill 20/4/35
Willesden 3/8/35
Crewe South 26/10/35
Aston 6/6/36
Walsall 11/7/36
Bescot 2/1/37
Aston 3/7/37
Bescot 25/9/37
Springs Branch 2/7/38
Rhyl 3/12/38
Llandudno Junction 8/4/39
Bangor 20/4/40
Llandudno Junction 25/6/49
Crewe South 1/10/49

Mileage at 12/36: 107,023
Mileage at 31/12/50: 481,771
Withdrawn w.e. 28/9/63
Cut up Horwich

Finale. 42984 in as good a condition as you'd find any freight loco, at Stockport Edgeley station on 4 May 1961. And looking as good too, despite the *unlined* tender! It was as well-travelled as any Stanier mogul, perhaps even more so, but after transfer to Crewe South in 1949, it was never stationed anywhere else. Photograph D. Forsyth, Paul Chancellor Collection.